WHAT'S ON SECOND?

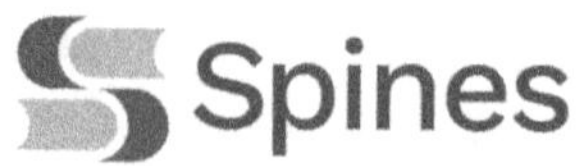

WHAT'S ON SECOND?

COMEDY WRITING FOR VENTRILOQUISTS

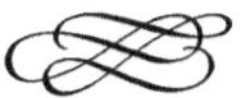

MLANJENI NDUMA

CONTENTS

Foreword   vii

Advisory Warning   xi

Acknowledgments   xiii

Part I
THE WRITING PROCESS

1. What Do You Write On That Line   3
2. Practice, Practice, Practice   4
3. Which Is Harder: The Stand-up Act Or The Ventriloquist Act?   6
4. Routing: Finding Your Comic Voice   9
5. On Creating Vent Dialogues   11
6. On Humor Through The Years   19
7. Other Forms Of Humor   21
8. On Hecklers And On Bombing   29

Part II
WRITING EXERCISES

9. FIND THE "FUNNY"   35
10. Finding Your Joke Groove   37
11. It Starts With You   40
12. Developing Characters   43
13. Understanding Empathy and Aesthetic Distance   47
14. Ad-libbing   57
15. Don't Forget The Visuals   60
16. Preparing The Jokes Into A Routine   62
17. On The Use of Ethnic Humor   70
18. Throw Aways… Adding The Spice   82
19. Rehearsing The Script   86

20. Finding Your Niche... Understanding Places   93
21. One Secret Of Performing For Children   96
22. The Ventriloquist Set List   98

Part III
A SAMPLE OF MY ROUTINES

23. Adult Routine   103
24. Children's Birthday Party   115
25. Christian Fellowship   129
26. Kwanzaa   141
27. Me and India Routine   150
28. Musical Introduction   161
29. The Banking Routine   165
30. The Tooth Fairy   173
31. The Writer   180

PART IV

32. Going Pro...There Is No Business Like
Show Business   187
33. My Conclusions   199

FOREWORD

I am African. My father's side is from Guinea. He was an African nationalist and passed on his pride and stride to me. I love performing now.

I was very shy growing up, but I started storytelling with puppets when I was five. I loved performing behind the puppet stage and wrote a lot of puppet plays through high school. In retrospect, I would say that only two were actually "good," but I was young. My heroes then were Shari Lewis, Paul Winchell and Lee Dexter. Two were puppeteers as well as ventriloquists, so I found a book at the library by Van Russler on Ventriloquism. I loved the pictures and I tried to do it. I wasn't satisfied with the results, but I was on my way. By junior high, my parents reluctantly bought me a Danny O'Day figure for Christmas. By high school, I had made my first figure and my dad actually let me perform my "act" and a bit of magic at one of his lodge dinners. I was terrified and delighted…terrified because one of my high school mates was in the audience! I stopped when I saw her there, but she whispered, "Keep going!" and away I went. Thanks Vickie!

By my mid-teen years, I joined the African freedom movement and became an officer in our war. I took a breather in college. I kept practicing, but I didn't perform. I just kept dreaming and planning. College was hard, but when I finally graduated I knew I had to get up on the stage again. I started working as a teacher in an African-American Freedom School in Harrisburg, Pennsylvania.. I began performing in the school and at birthday parties. I worked part-time at Hardee's and got to perform their customers' children's birthday parties as well. I left teaching to return to the big city of Philadelphia. I decided that this was the chance to go professional….and I've never looked back….okay, maybe once or twice, but not too much.

That's the essence of my story, but there was the other war side….but that stuff is not open to the public, although it has since been comic fodder.

In the course of being "on stage" I've done my fire-eating act, my psychic act, my magic acts, my stand-up comedy acts and my ventriloquist acts. I've directed plays at some local churches, taught theater and music at various community centers and continue to direct and work in the

Magical Theater which is a co-operative theater group which I founded. Now that the gray hair is coming in, I'm looking at going back behind the puppet stage as I have a few more stories to tell.

As a ventriloquist I prefer animal figures as I find them to be more versatile for my work than people figures....of course it could be that I grew up with Shari Lewis and Lee Dexter and their puppet stories. Paul Winchell's skits with Jerry and Knuckle Head required assistants to work their hands, much like the muppets. As a result, I've never ventured into that area. I've always performed the puppets and figures alone.

The figures, a suitcase, a small table, me and the audiences.....that's been my life as a ventriloquist.

ADVISORY WARNING

This book contains nuts…..well actually one nut, ME.

The routines contained in this book are real and have all been performed with the exception of one. I never did the **WEATHER APP** which is odd. I have no explanation, except that the dragon for the routine was lost in a fire. I've not had the time to rebuild him, so I just haven't done the routine yet.

All of the other jokes and joke samples have been in my stand- up routines or ventriloquist routines…. which means that they've come from some event that's happened in my life…. except for the one about the "Cruise-to-Nowhere." I'm too cheap to have given that to my parents!

The book is broken into four parts. There is a text which covers my history and experiences. There is a workbook which features exercises to help you develop your dialogue writing ability. The third part contains some of my routines. All of them have been performed. The forth part

is about my life as a professional and what one should expect.

ACKNOWLEDGMENTS

I'd like to acknowledge and thank all of those who helped make this little book possible.

No point in listing all the names….you know who you are. And a special thank you to the readers of the book as well.

Asante sana.

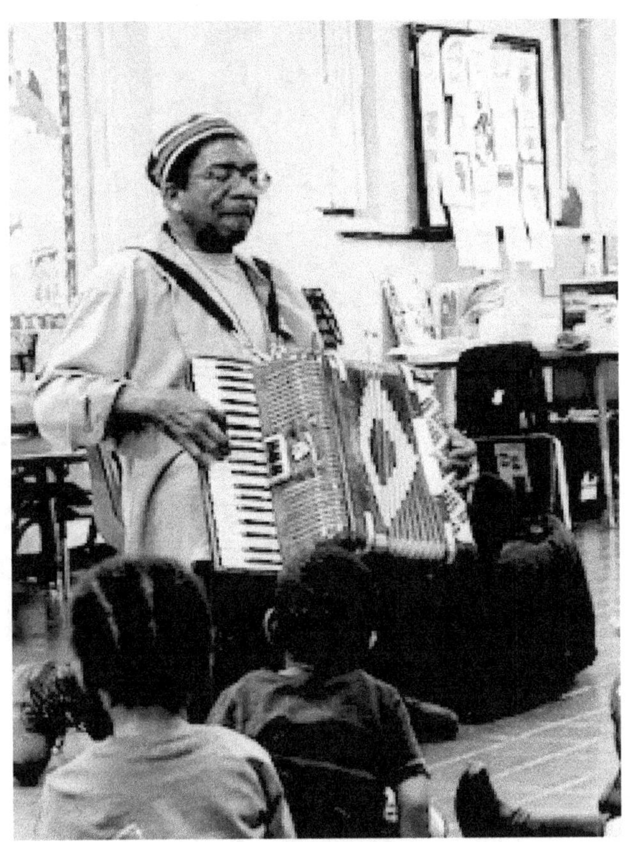

Mlanjeni Nduma

PART I
THE WRITING PROCESS

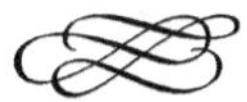

WHAT DO YOU WRITE ON THAT LINE

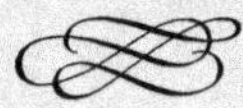

Your job application, whether it's with an agency, potential client, or audition form, asks simply "job title?" What do you write on that line? It takes a lot to write that one word: VENTRILOQUIST. I've written it, then erased it out of fear. It's easier to write "ENTERTAINER" than that one word because if you write it, you'd better be good at it! "VENTRILOQUIST."

PRACTICE, PRACTICE, PRACTICE

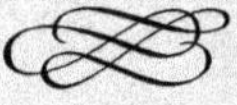

This little booklet is not a manual on learning the techniques of ventriloquism. It is not a teach-in on the methods. There are some great books on the hows... Paul Winchell's was my breakout favorite. Detweiler had a nice one as well. You can always check out Axtell's. There is nothing in this booklet about technique. No, this booklet will be covering an aspect of the art that is sorely lacking... writing scripts.

In terms of technique, you need voice control and lip control. These need practice. I personally view ventriloquism and conjuring (magic) as "circus" arts as opposed to "theatrical" arts such as acting, singing, or even dancing. Anyone involved in "circus" knows the necessity of daily practice... your life and the lives of those around you depend on it. If you are a wire walker, an acrobat, animal trainer, fire eater (me)... you know that missing a day of rehearsal has serious consequences. An actor or singer can take a week off; circus performers cannot. You absolutely have to practice "your act" daily. Ventriloquists, too, need to practice technique daily to stay on top of the game. I took a week off once, then got a call for a shoot (the Legacy Project). I was unprepared, and my lack of lip control for that hour remains on YouTube forever! I feel bad about it because I failed to create "the illusion." Ventriloquism as an entertainment is about creating an illusion, but that is not exactly what this booklet is about. The "illusion" aspect no longer stands alone. Ventriloquism "today" as entertainment is not just about skill but about "comedy," and that is what this booklet is about.

WHICH IS HARDER: THE STAND-UP ACT OR THE VENTRILOQUIST ACT?

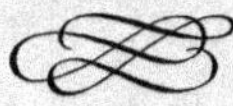

Both of these acts are a part of the comedy world... and I've been lucky (or unlucky) enough to have been a part of both. Orben put out a book many years ago entitled IF YOU HAVE TO BE A COMIC. While growing up, I personally found all of the Orben books to be hopelessly outdated. This is the only reference you'll find to an Orben book in this work... and yes, I found that book to be outdated too... but I loved and still love the title! IF YOU HAVE TO BE A COMIC... change it to IF YOU HAVE

TO BE A VENTRILOQUIST... it just says it all!

Some of us just don't have a choice in life. If you can be happy or unhappy, who would choose to be unhappy? Yet... who would choose a life which "could" go in that direction at any time? ... those of us in this comedy business! But when it's not "there" on the "unhappy," it's the greatest experience in the world! Comedians are not the happiest people, but we wouldn't trade the job for anything in the world! I can't think of any other job which is so aggravating and difficult (to me) and yet I can't walk away. I was made fun of growing up. My dad couldn't stand what I was doing. "He plays with dolls!" It hurt... yes! But I couldn't let it go. I had to be a comic! I had to be a ventriloquist! If you are in that category, this little book is for you.

Which is harder: the stand-up act or the ventriloquist act? They are both hard! It is hard to make a group of strangers laugh together. Your job is to go out and touch on the common experiences of people... to make them recognize their common humanity... to drop their guard against strangers and acquaintances enough to laugh out loud. That is your job as a comedian... whether you are solo or with your little friends.

As a stand-up comedian, the job of going out on stage is waaay harder than that of the ventriloquist. You are alone on that stage. If the audience is cold or if the jokes don't land that day, you are DONE! Crickets, jeers, or the host snatching your mike away... take your pick. There's nothing worse. Meanwhile, the ventriloquist can get smiles and laughs just by taking out a figure or puppet... it's weird, the audience automatically tunes itself to laugh. Every audience isn't great, but it's smoother sailing than the lone comic in the ring.

On the other hand, when it comes to writing material, the ventriloquist job is waaay harder than that of the stand-up comedian. As a comic, one has to be able to write material, i.e., jokes. As a stand-up, you are writing for yourself. As a ventriloquist, you have to be able to write dialogues for you and various partners. You are your own "writers' room!" Make no mistake about it, it is a tall order. This is one reason that many up-and-coming ventriloquists don't bother writing new material; they just use what already exists. Sad, sad, sad!

This little book is about understanding. Let's understand that if you just HAVE TO BE A VENTRILOQUIST, take the time to master not only the art but the comic aspects. You are a comedian... okay? You are a comedy team. Technically, you are the straight man/woman and your partner's the comedian. It's not an easy task. Master it!

ROUTING: FINDING YOUR COMIC VOICE

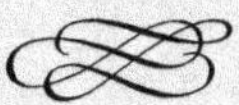

Most ventriloquists are amateurs or semi-pros, occasionally performing at church banquets, blue and gold banquets, schools, daycares, and events. Many of us have some nice figures and puppets which we manipulate well. Few of us have the "great" material that should accompany our "act." We are desperate for "great" material but often end up with the mediocre. We buy dialogues and use them or pieces of them to get "some" laughs, but usually not nearly enough. The rule is that a good comic has a laugh a minute in a club. Let's put it like this simply for you and your figure: "To be considered professional by your audience, your partner needs to get a smile a minute, a chuckle every two, and a full laugh every three." It's a tall order, but "old hat" jokes and techniques need to be worked on. I, for one, am tired of going on YouTube and watching some modern vents do jokes from

Paul Winchell's 1950s book, Edgar Bergen's 1940s material, Jimmy Nelson's Rag Mop (1950s), or even Abbott and Costello's 1940s Who's On First Routine... with no updates or improvements! WE CAN DO BETTER!

Contained within is some advice on how to improve material, revamp old material, and add a dash of spice to what you're doing. I am including some of my routines for your reading. Perhaps you'll laugh and find some pieces here that you can use in your work. Feel free to use whatever. The focus of this little pamphlet is "comedy." Ventriloquists in this day and time are expected to create laughter with a comedy "team" of figures and puppets.

ON CREATING VENT DIALOGUES

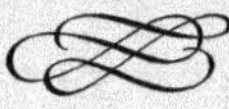

First, one must know how to write a joke. Then, one must know how to write for a partner. Characterization and dialogue are the key areas one must master to have a great act. There is really no separation; each is important.

WRITING JOKES

Start by reading as many jokes as you can. Read jokes every day. Go to your public library or bookstore. Read the jokes. These are generally what we call "stock" jokes. If you find some that make you laugh, write them down for future use.

Watch other comedians and comics. Note what makes you laugh and what doesn't. Try to figure out why a particular joke worked to get you to laugh and why one didn't. Note the various styles of the comics, and which styles appeal to you and which do not. This becomes important when trying out various styles with your puppets.

Read books on writing comedy... and practice writing jokes and comedy script ideas every day. I personally have a quota system... I write a minimum of two jokes every day plus attempt to create a daily visual joke. At the end of the week, I look over the jokes and throw out most of them... BUT there are always a few that I put in my official cataloged joke file. Normally, I find one of my written jokes really makes me laugh, and I'll imagine using it in a show... and from there I'll develop a set for the routine. A set is a series of jokes on one subject which one exhausts before going to another topic. This quota has led me to have hundreds of jokes in my file... the majority of my attempts are in the trash; I keep only the "gems." My rule is that if I don't laugh the next day when I read it — "it ain't funny!"... So into the trash it goes! If I laugh, it goes into the file. The files are alphabetical by subject.

I keep the visual jokes in a separate alphabetical file. Visual jokes come in handy when dealing with your figures and puppets. They are not always related to the comic routine. I remember one 45-minute set I had created for three puppets... I liked the routines, but they were strictly "B-level" material. They needed a little extra "something" to put them over the top... a "little something" for each puppet to do. The visual joke file helped immensely. I ended up giving one puppet a prop, one a new hat, and one some paper which he threw everywhere... The visual joke file was a lifesaver.

TYPES OF JOKES

I was always told that there are three basic types of jokes:

1. The standard reversal or what we'll call the HA HA!

2. The crazy joke or what we'll call the WHHAAT!

3. The topical or what we'll call the OUCH!

A good routine has all three types. In fact, the difference between a B-level routine and an A-level routine is the ability to have all three types in the complete act. Most of us have B-level routines, and if you are using routines from years ago (whether yours or someone else's), you have a B-level or C-level routine precisely because the material is old and dated. You've got to be able to create "topical" material to be a top-notch performer. It is that topical material that separates the A-level script from the B-level script.

Let's look at the jokes:

Here is the standard reversal or HA HA!

You start with a statement, then you turn it on its head. A straight line followed by the reversal or punch line, or a comic premise followed by a punch line.

(from "my first place" set)

I finally found a place. It wasn't great. It had a little bedroom, a little kitchen, a little bathroom and a BIG rent.

Those ROOMs Were so small, EVEN THE ROACHES WERE COMPLAINING.

****

I gave my parents an expensive anniversary gift... a cruise.....one of those "cruises-to-Nowhere".

I got ripped off....the boat never left the dock..

Watching a stand-up comedian helps you understand how to create patterns of jokes or "the set" – but doesn't really help with the creation of dialogues. That interaction with a partner is a whole different ball game.

V: I haven't seen you for a while, where have you been?

D: I got a new place.

V: Oh yeah? Where? How is it?

D: The first one was over on 4th. It wasn't great.....it had a little bedroom, and a little kitchen, and a little bathroom, and a BIG rent.

V: Oh?

D: Yeah. The rooms in that place were so small, even the roaches were complaining. So I had to take it up with that landlord....we had a big fight about it, then I got a new space.

V: Sometimes complaining works. How's the new space?

D: It was temporary, but it had a big kitchen, and a big bathroom and a nice size room, even a room-mate. Of course it also had lots of guards and bars in-between.

V: You were in jail?

D: Six months at county for assault.

Watch standard sit-coms and you can get a sense of rhythm of the "standard reversal" with two people talking...the set-up and the punchline. There was a time when comedians had "one liners", but today the tendency is to work a comic premise followed by a punchline. One liners in the tradition of Rodney Dangerfield or Johnny Carson are considered "very" old-school, hence hard to pull off in a successful act. "Two liners" are considered dialogue and continue to work well for ventriloquists and their partners. Your goal as a writer is to take the one liners and two liners and create a comic dialogue.

V: But doctor, I don't understand....why is it that it hurts when I touch my knee...it hurts when I touch my stomach....it hurts when I touch my forehead...what's wrong with me?

D: You have a fractured finger.

The Crazy: WHHAAT!

V: Kit, Kit is that you? (looking into the bag)

K: (slowly coming out) I think it's me...it was the last time I looked.....of course i could be wrong.

V: They invited us over. We're going to have some latkes.

K: latkes? Ugh!

V: do you know what a latkes is?

K: No, what's a latkes?

V: it's a potato pancake.

K: Ugh!

V: You like pancakes.

K: Yes, I love pancakes.

V: ...And you like potatoes.

K: No... I prefer french fries.

The Topical: OUCH!

You'll have to turn on your TV or Tablet or go to a comedy show for a sense of these. There's no point in my placing one here….it will be old within a month.

You can write topical jokes by reading your newspaper everyday and trying to find the jokes in the topics covered. The use of slang is also important to keep things topical. Audiences especially like it if you can include something local….but try to avoid making jokes about specific people in the audience even if they are local celebrities. I've tried it, the joke usually bombs! You don't know the person well enough to carry the joke over so just avoid it. If you don't believe me, go to YouTube and watch one of those Christian ventriloquists perform at a church function where he/she tries to engage a particular person, but clearly does not know the person or congregation….Sad - sad - sad! Jokes about local "places" work better than jokes about people you don't really know..

A topical joke comes off as relevant and "real." If you can create a scenario that seems current and real, you can create a "topical" joke which may keep its relevance for a while.

This joke is based on reality. It really happened, hence I'm placing it here as topical. My father has since passed on….and that reinforces the "temporary" nature of topical material.

My parents are aging. They've reached the point where they can't do for themselves like they used to so we have a home health care nurse come in once a month to look at them. So I'm telling her about them and one day she was concerned about my mental health. So she says that my mom and dad will change...they'll get cranky. They'll be demanding and they might pick on me ...just because. And I told her...they were always that way.

ON HUMOR THROUGH THE YEARS

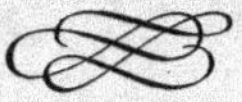

What is so annoying about most of the available "vent dialogues" is their age. Many are jokes from circa 1950-79. The problem is not that the jokes are not funny... indeed, vintage jokes can be funny to a collector of jokes, but not to a modern audience. Humor changes with each generation, and what was once funny becomes passé, lame, or downright offensive.

Stage humor within the U.S. hit its first stride within the old minstrel shows with "Negro" humor... and yes, that is where one can find the oldest one-and-two liners. Then came the vaudeville circuit, as well as the more "raunchy" burlesque circuit. The development of radio allowed "ethnic" humor to thrive... as well as the first famous radio ventriloquist, Edgar Bergen. Television led the way for the polished stand-up comic and the demise of the clownish/ethnic/minstrel comics... all of whom were on early television. Charlie McCarthy's radio and television routines are funny, but they still won't fly with today's audiences. A good example is from an episode of the Dean Martin Show (check out YouTube: Dean Martin, Edgar Bergen, and Charlie McCarthy). In this old clip, Dean is reprising the role of W.C. Fields in his interaction with McCarthy. It seems dated and stilted even then. In the early days of television, we had Paul Winchell's show and Shari Lewis' show. Again, funny stuff, but there are generational differences. Senor Wences' style of ventriloquism would have no chance with today's audiences... tricks are out unless merged with clever dialogue.

When working on your scripts, be aware of what humor is "in" and what is "out!" Drinking a cup of water while working might work for you depending on your figure, while smoking a cigarette is a definite "no." Sitcoms have changed over the years too, so be aware of the style of jokes that work. Although your act is not a "sitcom," it still follows the pattern in that you normally cover one or two subjects with your figure/puppet within a "situation." Some examples: "We just returned from a vacation..."; "The report card that you discovered"; "A first date"; etc.

OTHER FORMS OF HUMOR

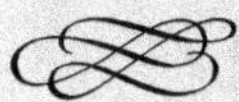

Social Commentary

Closely aligned with "Topical" humor is social commentary. This kind of humor is "generational" and works well when the audience is from the generation mentioned. Your social commentary jokes will last longer (a few years) than your topical jokes. The interplay between Jeff Dunham and Walter uses a lot of social commentary styled jokes.

I don't have any "social commentary" humor in my acts other than **THE TOOTH FAIRY** routine. (I don't want to just write a joke here as all of the jokes used in this manuscript have been worked and performed.)

Contemporary Cultural Icons

A good contemporary cultural icon will automatically garner a smile and a quick laugh as everyone has had the shared experience. These icons don't last forever, but if you know them particularly if visiting another city, you can get a solid laugh. There was a time when Comcast, AT & T, Kinko's, or Xerox were easy targets for laughs. The laugh comes from the shared experience of "poor" service. Movies and television shows that are either hated or adored are great as well.

I bought a table from ikea yesterday. I'm Still putting it together. Four legs and a top.....and I still have pieces left!

****

I've been binging out on the Nature channel..." When animals attack."

What a show! I've learned so much! Like languages. English has a word which we don't have in our traditional languages. The word "just"...we don't have that. This guy who works in Florida...his job is collecting golf balls from the lake. He gets 50 cents per ball. But this lake has an alligator in it...and the guy is like, "Well, it's just an alligator." Just? We do not have that word in our language! Just!

You don't go to one of our game reserves and hear a roar and someone says "Oh, it's just a lion."

In fact "everybody" in this show says the same thing after losing a leg, an arm, fingers...."Well, it was just a........bear, a shark, a cougar..." If anyone says to me "Well, it's just a ....." I'm out! I don't need to hear the rest!

I'm adding this word to our traditional language.... "Justa." It means "get the heck out of there! Run for your life!"

Political Humor.

There are some comedians who are adept at political humor, but very few ventriloquists venture down this road. Jeff Dunham has presented videos of his figures doing political "theater," mainly Walter pretending to be one of the presidents. He doesn't do it during his shows. Political humor is risky and can get one fired (Jimmy Walker's one political joke during his tour), or worse run out of the country (Kevin Hart during his Mexican tour). Personally, I do write political jokes as part of my joke writing exercises, but these jokes will never be a part of my shows....too risky! I do encourage you to write the material. WRITE, WRITE, WRITE! Who knows, you might be able to sell it...I just don't recommend using it for yourself or your partner.

Insult Humor

Insults can fly and laughs will follow as long as its between you and your partners. Insulting audience members with your partner can work if you are careful, keep it light and know who to pick on. My puppets and I have a running gag on my lack of musical ability.

V: And now to ring in the season, I will sing "Everywhere I Go, Everybody's Talking About Kwanzaa."

D: Wait! If everybody's 'talking' about it, why do we have to be tortured by you singing about it?

Song Parodies

I've never tried them with adults (Weird Al I'm not), but they work really well with children and family audiences.

OLD McDONALD (with Kit the dog)

V: Today we are talking about farming...

K: You know I once worked on a farm....the McDonald farm. I'm a farm dog.

V: You? The McDonald farm? You know Old McDonald?

K: ...That's Mrs. McDonald to you!

V: Mrs. McDonald? What happened to Mr. McDonald?

K: It's a long sad story. He's in (name a state).

V: Well how about we sing the old song, 'Old McDonald had a farm.'

K: Well, it wasn't exactly a farm...more like a garden.

V: Garden? How many acres?

K: What's an acre?

V: It's a form of measurement. How many yards was this garden?

K: It was one yard.

V: No, I mean how many feet did she have?

K: She had two feet.

V: Let's just sing...

K: Okay...(singing) Mrs. McDonald had a garden...

V: Eyah. Eyah. Ooooh. K: No. No. No.

V: No?No? No?

K: No. No. No. She never liked that 'Eyah. Eyah. OO.' stuff. Just sing, 'And a wonderful garden it was.'

V: (singing) ....and a wonderful garden it was....you sing it.

Mrs. McDonald had a garden.....

K: ....and a wonderful garden it was...... V: And in this garden there was a cow.....

K: no.no. no.

V: No. No. No?

K: No.No. NO. she never had a cow....she never liked cows. Too noisy.

V: Okay, we'll start over....'Mrs. McDonald had a

garden.

K: ....and a wonderful garden it was......

V: in this garden she had a duck...

K: No. No. No.

V: No? No? No?

K: No. No. No. She never liked ducks....too noisy.

V: What about ***Chickens?***

K: No.

V: Too noisy?

K: No, too nosey!

V: Well, what did she have?

K: She had some tomatoes. She liked those... (the dialogue ends with the children singing)

Poems and Puns

Puns don't go over very well in the U.S.A. I'm not sure about poems either. I don't like poetry! (Okay, that's a long sad story....I once had a relationship with a budding national poet. My relationship became the subject of her work for a full year and was published all over the place... then came the break-up...also published all over the place! I hate poets!)

But back to puns....they are "out" in the U.S.A.

Sketch Comedy

A good sketch comedy piece really adds to a show as something of a novelty change of pace. There are those ventriloquists who use two audience members as figures/puppets in their shows providing the comic voice as "he and she" open their mouths in some comic situations. Ken Groves does it at the Amish Theater. There are also vents who create a sketch with their figures...such as David Straussman and Chuck Wood doing their psychic act or Otto and George reenacting the Kennedy assassination. I believe that Paul Winchell's Dentist sketch could still work if presented right on stage with you and your figure each taking a role and dressing in front of the audience. I've never done it, but sketch comedy seems to work fine for quite a few.

ON HECKLERS AND ON BOMBING

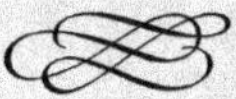

I've never consistently worked the type of venues where one could get heckled (bars and clubs) … My audiences have always been supportive and pleasant. I have done stand-up solo, so I do know about bombing! Nothing is more annoying than hearing those "crickets" on stage. THANKFULLY, I'm a ventriloquist! These days I always carry a puppet on stage in a bag ready to go. Whenever I start bombing with stand-up, I take out the puppet. People like the puppets! Whatever antics the puppets do, a laugh is sure to follow — so my advice as a ventriloquist – don't worry about BOMBING unless you are going for the nightclub and bar scene! Just try to keep your vent act fresh and entertaining …and keep some topical stuff in it too! YOU'LL BE FINE!

If the jokes with your figure aren't working at a particular gig, just switch over to "skill". This is the point where you show your ventriloquial skill … .drink that glass of water with your figure talking, do the tongue twisters or sing that tongue twister song, use the distant voice, anything that shows off your skill. When you are done, you'll still get that applause!

My hardest venues occurred during the 2020 covid-19 pandemic. All of our shows during that time were VIRTUAL. We were still developing a technical sense of how to do a VIRTUAL show, and one thing that was definitely missing was the laughter. There was that video delay between the broadcast and the response from the audience so our comic timing was completely off. OUCH! I was so glad when the LIVE shows came back!

There was the day I nearly bombed, but for the skill of practicing. It came when I was the last minute substitute performer for a children's birthday party. The agency booked a 30 minute set for a "balloon artist." The artist canceled. I can do balloon animals along with the ventriloquism, so I was asked to go. Intuition told me to take my traditional Djembe drummer along…follow your intuition! We arrived expecting 20 children and found only 4. It was not a children's party at all! It was an adult party, and the birthday "child" was 65. She was the host, and threw the party for herself! Needless to say I was unprepared for the event. Fortunately my drummer began the rhythms and my puppet dog appeared. I had no jokes for this event.…but my dog Kit has been a part of my shows for years. He is so much a part of my subconscious, that he knows where the jokes are in my head! He started working the crowd, ad-libbing everything. The adults were laughing and the host was delighted! She gave me a 5 star review. Practicing dialogues, ad-libbing in rehearsals, knowing and loving your little partners is essential. It saved me that day from bombing! I practice lip-control everyday…but the writing and spontaneous dialogues are important too!

PART II
WRITING EXERCISES

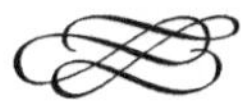

The rules are simple:

Find the "funny."

Keep a journal of some kind. Keep a joke file.

Write 2 jokes everyday.

FIND THE "FUNNY"

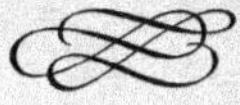

Laughter is most times a shared experience.

We live on a planet. Our planet Earth goes around the sun as it swirls around the galaxy. The planet is full of events, as is your life. Everyday take a moment to reflect on this… what did you see today? What did you do today? Within these things and events, you need to find the "funny." Look for it, and write it down in your journal. If other mammals can find it….and if you've had a dog or cat, you know they know how to find it when they laugh and smile at you….you need to find it too. If it makes you smile or chuckle, write a line about it in your journal. It may seem like a senseless exercise (much like in

High school), but this exercise helps you focus on the little things that make one laugh. These observations can often be the basis of a joke set.

Observation: The Sunday comics were called "funnies"…but they're not funny.

FINDING YOUR JOKE GROOVE

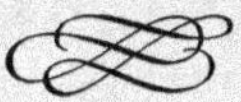

You must keep a joke file of some kind. You need this to find jokes when you need some. You take a risk if you think that you can remember every joke you've ever come across. Write down jokes that you create; write down jokes that make you laugh and credit them to whoever said it in your file. Keep the file in some order in which you can easily reference it. You can find jokes in joke books, on sitcoms, and in everyday situations. (I'd say in newspaper comics, but as noted, they tend to be very lame.) The larger your file becomes, the easier it is to put your vent act together. Your act should be made of sharpened or switched jokes, "new" original jokes and "context" humor.

Sharpened or switched jokes are jokes from your file. These are old jokes that you are recycling with a few touches to bring it up to today….

The original: **_WHY DID THE CHICKEN CROSS THE ROAD?_**

TO GET TO THE OTHER SIDE.

Henny Youngman's change: **_WHY DID THE CHICKEN CROSS THE ROAD?_**

THAT WAS NO CHICKEN, THAT WAS MY WIFE.

My switch below isn't much of a switch, but it could lead into a set....

V: Why did the chicken cross the road?

D: Are you losing it? 'Why did the chicken cross the road?' Who cares! I don't even know the last time I saw a chicken! (shout to audience) Hey, did anyone see a chicken cross the road lately? Bird Brain here wants to know why they cross the road.

New "original" jokes are the ones you create through your observations, and experiences.

"Context humor" is the series of jokes that you pull together subconsciously from your "joke memory" and from your experiences on a specific topic. You'll know it when you feel it! Basically it means "you're on a roll" when writing. You will just start laughing as you're writing the jokes to the set.

Note the set reflects the changes in humor over the years. Currently (2024) context humor is in play as opposed to the old straight line - punch line format. AND that's fine as long as it still generates A SMILE - A CHUCKLE OR A LAUGH.

These are your creations. Find your comic groove, you can write new jokes. You'll find that these new ones are most often topical.

Writing jokes takes practice.....

EVERYDAY….PRACTICE WRITING.

My minimum joke quota is two verbal and one visual daily.

Most of them will be trashed, but write them anyway. (Note: My example above….

"Bird brain here wants to know why…." is just that– an example. Would I use it in my act? It's unlikely since it wouldn't get into my joke file. It's cute, but it doesn't make me chuckle.)

IT STARTS WITH YOU

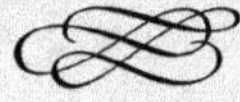

Finding the jokes starts with you. Great comedy comes from within.

An exercise:

Let's start with things that have happened to you last week. Take a moment and write down four events that happened to you last week.

***My real life examples:* :**

A. Thanksgiving family dinner with foods that no one ate….

My vegan sister's foods and my gourmet mother's foods

B. The dog dragged me into a pond again

C. My niece thinks that she's my boss, and that I'm sexist for not giving her the power

D. I'm traveling…it's 5:00 am and I have an Uber driver who won't stop talking on my way to the train station.

You will notice that some of the "things" that happened are funny in and of themselves. You will find these on your list as well. You now have some subjects to make into jokes.

Pick one…….Bring out your (stock) joke books and start looking for related topics. Go to your joke file and see what you've listed.

Here's my real life example…..I'm creating as I type this….. Thanksgiving….hmm. Never liked it since the relatives always come over. (Start creating)…which relatives and why I don't like them… jokes.

Foods…..tofu turkey! Egg plant! ….start looking for ridiculous foods that no one would eat. Lots of funny here…..

F: You vegans are so picky. You can't use a pot that had meat in it! 'Don't touch the egg with that spoon!' 'What's in that Gravy?'

V: Hey, the question is 'Did you like the food?' Did you enjoy the dinner?

F: Not really. I developed a nut allergy.

V: Really? Allergic to nuts? Peanuts?

F: No, allergic to 'people - nuts' …..like you.

I'm traveling….could combine the traveling with my Thanksgiving to add more to the routine….I hate talky drivers.

Noticing a lot of "hate this" and "hate that"….this could be great for the interaction between my figure and I with one of us "loving" the holiday and the other "not-so-much."

DEVELOPING CHARACTERS

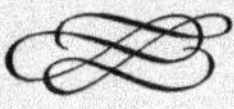

There are two parts to developing a vent act. One is the dynamics between the vent and the puppet/figure, and the other is the jokes. Each is important. A vent act is not a series of jokes between a ventriloquist and his/her figure. It is a dynamic relationship, and that relationship fuels the humor. What the puppet/figure says is not always funny. In fact if you only read a script, you might miss the laughs. It is often the manipulation of the figure, the voicing and/or the context that brings the laughs. My puppet dragon, Ijangayanga will stop talking mid-sentence, pause, and then just tilt his head sideways....it always gets a chuckle. Building characterization is essential for an act.

FINDING YOUR CHARACTERISATION

There is not much I can say about characterization as I assume if you are reading this little manual, you already have your figure/puppet. What is important is that you find not only your puppet's characterization, but your own. There has to be a contrast between you two. If you are using more than one puppet/figure in your set, your character has to be consistent as well. Look at Jeff Dunham and his interaction with his figures. Contrast that with Nina Conti and her figures. Check out David Strassman and his figures. Each ventriloquist presents himself/herself differently, yet all are fantastic! How does one develop the characters?

Start with your figure's biography. Write it down and stick to it. Birthday, home town, hobbies, school, etc. Now write out your own biography relative to your puppets, i.e. your character on stage does not have to be "you!" A fictionalized you is just as acceptable…provided you stick with it onstage. Look at Edgar Bergan…he always seemed somewhat posh and possibly British onstage….or was that on radio!

Once you have your two biographies down, sit with your figure/puppet, pick a subject and just talk. Let each of you stay in character; you don't have to be funny here….just get used to talking about things of interest to one or both of you. You might even stumble upon a joke, but the point of this exercise....which you should do at least once a week....is to establish a relationship and a rhythm. This becomes important as you perform....your figure comes alive around you and eventually will be able to ad lib in situations. Ijangayanga the dragon is my oldest figure. We had many gigs at Children's Hospital of Philadelphia ... .the dragon was much loved by the staff as after the storytelling sessions he interacted with the children and created much laughter. All of his dialogues were ad libbed...as noted by the staff...yet they were always appropriate for the situations. According to the staff, many of the children we visited had not smiled or laughed during their stay until they ran into that dragon! Once you have the characterization of your figure down, it becomes subconscious and the responses become spontaneous. All pro ventriloquists can give you stories of their puppets answering questions from others before he/she consciously could ... .the figure just blurts it out! Try the "talking about anything" exercise weekly.....you'll see the harvest eventually.

I had read a great french book on comedy the name of which I have forgotten...the book perished in a fire. What I really learned from the book was the connection between tragedy, comedy and characterizations. Basically the author pointed out that comic characters have a tragic flaw which makes the audience realize that they are better than the character. This character's flaw creates the situations that escalate into a crisis. The other characters help to resolve the crisis, but the resolution doesn't lead to a lesson or epiphany for the flawed character. He or she continues with the same mindset....and that is the reason he or she is so beloved by the audience. The sitcom Curb Your Enthusiasm is a perfect example of this...the Larry David character and his myopic worldview were most beloved and the audience returned again and again to watch the character in new adventures. Of course Punch of Punch and Judy has been breaking norms and heads for over a hundred years. What "tragic flaw" does your figure or puppet have? Find one.

UNDERSTANDING EMPATHY AND AESTHETIC DISTANCE

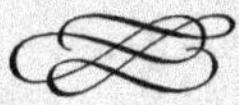

The audience must like the characters in front of them. Empathy means that they see a little of themselves or someone close to them in you and your figures, hence they can relate to what is being said. Everyone knows someone like Jeff Dunham's Walter. People relate to Nina Conti's smart sassy monkey because he says what we think but can not say in this civilized society. Empathy.

Aesthetic Distance in comedy means knowing when to bring something up. **"Too soon!"** is a real thing in comedy. Notice in the exercise, I said 'think of things that happened to you Last week.' That "last week" provides aesthetic distance to your thinking. It exists for the audience as well. If you had a car crash yesterday and someone was hurt, you can't make a joke about it today. (A 911 emergency operator in Philadelphia received jail-time for making such a joke…..she should have waited a week!)

Sept. 11th happened and the late Gilbert Godfried made a joke about it —too soon! Was the response. He got fired from his Aflac insurance duck job for something similar after the Japanese tsunami. When creating material, know when you can look at events in your own life and find the humor without feeling trauma. Know when you can joke about national events without creating anger in your audiences also. Do write the jokes anyway, just know when to use them. The easiest exercise in writing for tragic events is the old "Well, I have good news and bad news" format.

F: Well, your doctor just called about your visit. He wanted you to know that there's good news and bad news.

V: What's the good news?

F: They're going to name the disease after you.

V: and the Bad news?

F: He wants all of his money before Friday.

or

F: (who's having a bluetooth phone call)

Hmmm. Hmmm. Tell her to calm down!

V: What's wrong?

F: My grandma's having a panic attack on a plane….some kind of turbulance….What's that Grandpa?….Oh…the pilot's coming on over the intercom……Oh he's saying 'There's good news and bad news'……….

V: What's the good news?

F: ……the airlines going to pay for all of the funerals…..

V: And the bad?

F: …..they're about to be buried at sea!

As I'm writing this (late 2023) the terrorist group Hamas has attacked Israel and Israel has responded with an attack on Gaza. This is a tragic event on all sides….BUT I still have to write the jokes. Will I use them?…. Don't ask! I chuckled so they could be in!

From the Israeli side:

Says the Israeli troop to a father…

" Well sir, there's good news and bad news."

"What's the good news?"

"You won't be seeing your mother-in-law for a while."

From the Palestinian side:

Says the Hamas landlord to a resident:

"Yasir, I have good news and bad news."

"What's the good news?"

"You won't be complaining about the leaky roof anymore."

Meanwhile, back to me.....I'm looking at event D.

V: I can't believe you got us kicked out of that Uber today!

F: Hey, it was 5 in the morning, and he wouldn't shut up!

V: Did you have to aggravate him?

D: All I said was 'If you could drive as fast as your mouth is moving, we'd be in (nearby state) already!'

This is a weak joke. It doesn't work....I'm running through states in my head and nothing!

But there's a Christmas tree here in my niece's place....so what if my little friend is rushing me into the city to see Santa Claus at Macy's......

I change the punch line to:

All I said was 'If you could drive as fast as your mouth is moving, we'd be at the North Pole! The North Pole!

And I smile…..perfect! I smiled…..remember A SMILE, A CHUCKLE OR A LAUGH is the goal. If it works for you it MIGHT work for your audience. The joke goes into my joke file along with a note that the routine will be a Christmas seasonal one.

****

Okay so you're keeping a joke file.

Okay, so you're writing everyday.

Okay, so you're listening to jokes on your tablet, telephone, or TV.

Okay, so here's an exercise…..

Take out your joke books….if you don't have any, go buy some!

Read a joke and try to switch it from a one liner into a two liner…from a joke to a dialogue.

This is a hard exercise, but again, the more you do it, the better you get at it. Every joke will not fit your style, so think of your favorite vents and their figures and imagine them using the joke. Try a few for yourself…. In time you'll hear your partner in your head making the lines work.

Here's a joke from Harry Allen's "Sleight of Mouth" * changed into a two liner:

(Sleight of Mouth is a great book of one liners primarily for magicians to use)

V: Well, everyone, I am pleased to say that I have performed for four presidents.

P: What? That performance last week in front of Mount Rushmore doesn't count! You will see that one in one of my routines. And after reading his jokes on "mistakes in magic" trickery, I came up with this:

P: I want you to help me with my magic trick so I can keep my hands clean.

V: You mean this trick is messy?

P: No. I just need you so I have someone to blame if it doesn't work.

Some jokes are one liners; some are stories with a punchline; some are songs or puns ... .no matter, just try to make them into dialogues with an imagined partner. If you think they are worth saving....put them in your joke file! Just don't forget to keep order in the file so you can find it if you need it!

Real life example: 4 Oct. 2022

It's been raining for a few days….I've been getting wet thanks to a ridiculously "bad" weather app…..I've talked about this app with other people and they've agreed…it's bad! When my joke creation time came (walking the dog) I came up with this which I've put in my joke file. I was thinking about the comedy team Roland and Martin as I tried to create it. It has their style and rhythm in my mind. (Feel free to use or change as desired)

DIALOGUE WITH COUSIN KOMODO, THE DIM-WITTED COUSIN OF IJANGAYANGA

V: (looking at my phone talking to myself) I hate this weather app "IC-IC."

K: I see what?

V: Nothing. I'm just talking to myself about this weather app. It's the worst! I just need to know if it's going to rain tomorrow.

K: You want to know the weather? You've come to the right place! "Weather dragon" at your service.

V: You know the weather?

K: Absolutely, positively!

V: I'm having an event, I need to know….is it going to rain tomorrow?

K: Tomorrow.....which tomorrow are you talking about?

V: What do you mean 'which tomorrow?' There's only one tomorrow...tomorrow. Today is ____________ and tomorrow is __________.

K: Well, yeah, but yesterday, tomorrow was today, ____________.

V: Do you mind. I just want to know if it's going to rain tomorrow. Are you a weatherman?

K: I'm a weather dragon.

V: Well, is it going to rain tomorrow?

K: Let me see...Yeah, it could rain tomorrow.....then again, it might not.

V: Is it going to rain or not?

K: It might....and then again, it might not.

V: Well, what's the probability of rain tomorrow?

K: The probability is about 50-50.

V: Thanks, that's great....what's the temperature? Is it going to be hot or cold?

K: It's going to be hot....or cold....depends on the weather.

V: Do you know anything about the weather? What's the humidity?

K: Who?

V: The humidity.

K: Oh, never met him.

V: It's not a 'him!'

K: Oh I'm sorry, never met 'her.'

V: The humidity is the water in the air! Is there going to be humidity?

K: Water in the air? Oh you mean is it going to rain…well it might….then again it might not!

V: Can't you make a commitment! I just want to know if it's going to rain tomorrow.

K: Well, I'll tell you….YES, it's going to rain tomorrow.

V: Thank you….are you positive?

K: Now wait, only fools are positive.

V: Well, are you sure?

K: Yeah…. I'm positive!

V: What do I have to lose, you can't be any worse than this IC-IC weather app.

K: You're using the IC-IC weather app?

V: Yes…

K: Hey, I invented that….small world, ain't it?

This little set has all the joke types….it performs funnier than it reads as the characters interact.

THE LESSON: It takes jokes AND characterization to create a set.

AD-LIBBING

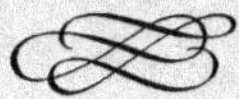

Children love the figures and puppets when they engage them in conversations. They love talking to the puppets. When the puppet looks at them and speaks directly to an individual child or group, that special attention creates joy….which is evident on their faces. One need not create jokes when ad-libbing with children, just asking for the names, asking about things makes the children smile and laugh. Adults experience the same reaction, but adults expect the figures and puppets to be "funny." Hence one must be good at ad-libbing jokes. I think Nina Conti is the best at this, so the exercises that I propose recognize how she does it.

Most ad-libs will come when the figure selects someone to talk to. The figure or puppet will invariably ask one's name, job or place of residence. Their answer becomes the basis of the ad-lib. So there are two parts to learning how to ad-lib: 1.) knowing your puppet's character well enough and 2.) having an encyclopedic memory file of stock jokes on names, jobs and places.

Your puppet/figure must be able to respond quickly to the person's comment or answer. Your strongest or most experienced puppet is the one to use for your ad-libbing. The answer will come across as "natural." The creation of "an encyclopedic memory file" is a bit harder, but here is the exercise that will help. If you want to be good at ad-libbing, every day go to a McDonalds, or get on a bus or train and look around at the people. Pick one person. Guess what job he or she has; guess his or her name; guess where this person is from. Write these on a card and in the course of the day, write a joke about their name, their job or their place. If you can't come up with anything, go to your (stock) joke books and find something you can use. Put it on the card and file it. If you do this exercise everyday, you will get good at it and you'll eventually have that encyclopedic memory file. You yourself will be amazed at how quick your figure/puppet will interact and ad-lib when hearing someone's answer about their name, job, etc.

F: What do you do? You're a surgeon? Wow.

V: That's a nice job. Important.

F: My uncle was a surgeon… A tree surgeon. He had to give it up.

V: Give it up? Why?

F: The trees wouldn't pay.

DON'T FORGET THE VISUALS

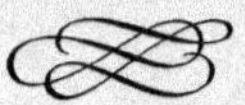

Visual humor is important in your act as well. I'm talking about standard stock visual jokes between you and your figure. Know them and use them….these won't have your audience rolling in the aisles, but they will get that smile and a chuckle. I must assume that you know these, they've been around for centuries! Just remember to use them.

For you the ventriloquist:

The slow burn…your eyes glare; your lips curl; you ball your fist; you turn your head and glare.

The double-take…you look at something; look at the audience then look at it again.

The dead pan….you stare ahead; your eyes go up then come down; you stare ahead again.

For your partner:

The shock and drop…his/her mouth falls open; eyes close and figure faints backwards.

The sad-sad-sad (a/k/a " I can't believe you said that)....head looks down and shakes "no, no, no."

The "I'm out!"... where he or she nearly gets off your knee or out of the seat to leave..

PREPARING THE JOKES INTO A ROUTINE

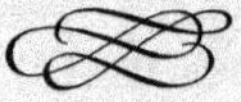

A routine is the 10 - 15 minute set that you have with one of your figures. It is that string of jokes on one or two topics. To begin you pick a topic. Write it at the top of a page. Leave some space then write PEOPLE…….PLACES/SPACES………..THINGS ……..AND WHATEVER. As you think about your topic, write down anything and everything that comes to mind about it under each word category. No sentences (yet), just words or phrases that relate to the topic. When you're done, take another sheet of paper and go through the list writing notes, sentences or jokes about each thing you've written under each category. This exercise takes a while. Don't rush it, just let the ideas flow.

It can take hours or days.

As noted in the first section, there are different kinds of jokes....but they all have the same format. There is the set up followed by the punch line. Some jokes require a long set-up and some do not. We ventriloquist do not generally use jokes with long set-ups. The interaction with your figures is very basic....set-up lines followed by the punch lines. When looking at your stock joke books, if you see a long paragraph joke, don't even think about using it unless you can break it into segments. If you can break it up and fill it up with smaller jokes, that joke could be your climax. Otherwise, it probably won't work for your routine. Stick to the basics.

Okay examples.....the late, great Red Skelton has a number of LONG set-up jokes....hilarious stuff. (Thanks YouTube.) The late Norm McDonald is another comedian who can tell a long set up joke...and get the laugh when the punchline finally comes. Micheal Colyar is another. (The late) Rodney Dangerfield and (the great) Jerry Steinfield tell basic format jokes...one liners. As ventriloquists we must have two liners. So one must be able to change those one liners into two liners.

Let's look into a joke: a stock joke...

When I was young, I was very poor.

And now after years of effort..... I'm old.

This is an interesting joke. Not every comedian can tell it and get the laugh even if he or she is old.

This one takes a certain timing…that pause… to make the punch line work.

Punch lines require a certain rhythm or a "turn" of the words. Saying one requires practice "outloud." It is weird how much time you may spend just repeating the joke just to get that punchline right, but practice you must! My family thinks that I'm insane because I spend time "talking" to myself. They don't know that I'm practicing the pacing of the punchline.

Now let's look at the joke as a two liner…..

V: When I was young, I was very poor.

D: And now, after years of effort….you're old!

A weak joke.

But it could get a smile or a chuckle from my partner's audience if he/she makes that "pause" work….

F: And now after years of effort….(looks me up and down…slowly shakes head)…..you're old!

Personally, I think the joke needs a better punch line to be a two liner. Let's try another….

V: When I was young, I was very poor.

F: And now, after years of effort.....you're still poor!

I just smiled....so it's in! Here's a real time example of creating a routine.....(Spring 2024)

I start thinking of how this could be a conversation about investing my money in some scheme that my partner has cooked up. Thus begins a "routined topic." I look through my joke file for

"investments", banks, odd jobs, anything that may relate to me investing in something. If I can string these jokes together, I might have the beginnings of a routine. PEOPLE...............PLACES............... THINGS.................AND? (anything coming to mind)

****

Here goes my **Real time example** as I'm writing this......

I'm looking over the word list, then the phrases and then "Voila!" .....jokes about the PLACE.

V: Good evening ladies and gentleman. It's wonderful to be here today.

F: Right. What a dump!

V: What? You don't walk into somebody's space and call it a dump. It's rude. It's crude. You didn't even say 'hello.'

F: Oh, excuse me....Hello. How's everybody doing? Good....this place is a dump! I hope we're getting paid for this.

V: What's wrong with you? What do you care if we're getting paid? You're always worried about money. You don't see me worried about money.

F: Yeah, that's the problem....YOU don't worry about money. I have needs!

V: What, another video game? That's the problem with your generation, you don't know sacrifice...you don't know struggle. When I was young, I was very poor...but after years of effort....

F: You're still poor.

V: I don't like to say... 'poor,'... I live... 'comfortably.'

F: Yeah, YOUR fancy way to say..... 'Poor.'

****

Looking it over, it's not too shabby. It takes a certain kind of figure to make it work AND I'm confident that it will work as it makes me smile, chuckle and laugh as I read it. (Before I publish this book, LET'S finish this routine and work it in front of an audience for the PART 3 collection.)

I put my thinking cap on and think about the topics in play....

TOPIC: INVESTING/ RICHES/ POVERTY

PEOPLE: bankers, investment managers, bank tellers, judges

PLACES: court, the bank, wall street, the corner

AND?: a lemonade stand, 3 card monte, bankruptcy, pyramid scheme,

Now I try to find jokes to match every one of the topics, people, places and AND?

I'll put them on 3x5 cards....

****

String the jokes together in some type of logical order to create the routine. The routine must have a climax. The climax is the last joke...this is the one that indicates that you've exhausted the subject with your figure/puppet. It must get the biggest laugh for that topic and ends the set with the figure. You will have to shift the jokes around to find it and you'll find it with trial and error. I had that great stand-up bit on "When animals attack" in the middle of my set. My joke with a bear eating people after praying got the biggest laugh, hence it goes to the end of the routine. Trial and error. As you perform the routine in front of an audience, you will feel what jokes work best, which don't work and which should climax your routine in time. Switch the jokes around until you're satisfied…then it's comic gold!

Let's look at the example again.

Let's keep it simple…we're going to use the example above and finish the routine. This will be a real time example…..I'm going to let you see the process I use to develop it. At this point I'm not sure that a routine can be developed, but whatever happens you'll see the process.

It's 12 Jan. 2024. I want a routine on investing….it's 5:30 am and I'm cursing myself for accepting this challenge. Why did I agree?….I don't know anything about investing! (This is the norm for me when I accept a booking for something I know nothing about…..like my ME AND INDIA ROUTINE.

11:00 am. I'm walking the dog and working on the script. I need some kind of context to make it work. I'm thinking Edgar Bergan and Charlie McCarthy since scheming to get some money would be a Charlie McCarthy kind of thing. The initial dialogue seems like his style also….so if it were Bergan, he would admonish Charlie with some type of story…..I like the idea! A story about what? Frugality. …perhaps a Ben Franklin story…who's more frugal than Ben Franklin. The idea of using Ben Franklin opens a lot of doors….the whole colonial era with it's names, places and oddities and France too. …Perfect!

Wait! African-American slavery occurred during Franklin's era along with the massacre of the First Nation's peoples. DRAT! NOW WHAT?

ON THE USE OF ETHNIC HUMOR

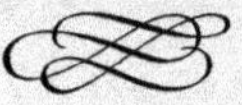

You have to know your niche as a comic! You will have an appeal to certain types of audiences and you need to be clear on who they are. You need to know how far you can go in your set to maintain commercial success. As a comic I believe that any topic is fair game, but I also know better than to try it! I am not Jewish, so I do not do jokes about the Holocaust. I am not transgender, so I do not do jokes about transgender people. I am African (American), so I have done jokes about slavery….because I can without fear of overstepping and offending. If you work in a narrow niche, you may be successful at it. I look at the late Otto and George's act. Their niche was basically "Frat-boy/Bro culture" male audiences. Their act was hilarious, yet highly offensive if you were not a part of that demographic! But wow! Hilarious! The downside is that their act was never mainstream and could never go mainstream. There was an X-rated African-American ventriloquist act also….but I can't remember who it was….and that's my point! Narrow niches can be lucrative, but in the long run be leery of the narrow niche markets. The internet keeps your history. I like Disney so I like to be squeaky- clean and inoffensive. I like to be able to perform anywhere and anytime without worry. I remember an anecdote from my father about one of his lodge members…. This guy was so profane. Every other word was a profane one. The lodge had their annual service in a church and this guy was asked to pray. He couldn't because he knew if he started talking/praying what words would come out of his lips. He broke down, fell on his knees and cried…or so I was told. I never want to be in that spot!

But I digress…. Let's go back. The jokes…..let's just stick to Franklin himself and his pithy statements. It's 9:00 pm. 01/12/24

Names: Benjamin Franklin………Benny Franklin

And?……switches on American proverbs…..''an apple a day——- will keep you on the toilet. A penny saved is——----- the sign of a cheapskate.''

Thoughts:

F: Ben Franklin? Of course I know Ben Franklin! Old Benny! I can channel ol' Benny!

F: Investments? I've got good news and bad news…

V: What's the good news?

F: That stock that cost ten dollars a share shrank down to a penny a share!

V: Good news? How is that good news?

F: At least there's still something.

V: And the bad news?

F: I used your credit card to buy 50 shares the other day.

****

Sat. 01/13/24 I thought of and threw out some jokes today….these are the ones that made me smile…the rest are trashed.

V: Perhaps you need to learn a lesson from Ben Franklin.

F: Benny Franklin? You know Benny Franklin?

V: Benny? Is this the Ben Franklin with the pithy statements? Like 'A penny saved is a penny earned.'

F: A penny? That ain't Benny. He said 'An apple a day….will keep you on the toilet.'

V: Ben Franklin was in a band of patriots…the American Revolution.

F: No. He's the lead guitar in the band Stars and Stripes.

V: Ben Franklin lived in 1776, the American Revolution.

F: And you knew him? No wonder you're standing here talking about pennies….you're old!

V: The man was very wise…'A penny saved is a penny earned!'

F: We don't do pennies, we do CashApp.

F: Benny Franklin. He's my Uber driver. You should meet him. He'll show you how to invest your money.

V: Right, an Uber driver.

F: He's an investment banker by day.

V: But he drives an Uber at night. How successful can he be?

F: This…. from someone who saves… pennies?

****

I'm thinking about Ben Franklin and how he represented the early Congress around Europe. I'm thinking of how the British visiting the states then made fun of the colonial Americans…..they called them Yankee Doodles. Maybe I could bring it up… maybe my partner could sing the song to end the routine. I'll have to look up the song though, I don't remember it.

****

01/14/24 10:00pm.

Here's todays jokes for this script:

F: He's an investment banker. He was in the bank one day when it got robbed.

V: What?

F: Yeah, guy demanded all the money....'put it in a bag and hand it over.'

V: Was he scared?

F: No, according to him, he didn't flinch.

V: Well, he was lucky and brave.

F: Yeah, that's just what the police said ......when they arrested him outside. Said he was lucky that explosive packet hadn't gone off.

V: Your friend is a bank robber? I thought he was an investment banker.

F: He is...he knows how to invest money. You can meet him in about 10 years.

****

01/15/24 11:00pm

F: You really need to give my guy Benny a chance. He can find you some good investments.

V: No thanks, I don't know him.

F: I've got a question for you….why is it that a person that invests their own money is called 'An investor.' But if that person invests your money, his money or her money, he's a 'broker.'

V: I don't know and that sure doesn't make me want to trust your guy.

F: You can trust my guy. He's lucky and brave. He was in the bank one day when it got robbed…..

****

I try to work on this routine everyday.

Sometimes there's a few good jokes; sometimes there's only one. That's the nature of joke writing. Write every day. Some days are fruitful and some less so. Don't go to bed though without creating at least one good one! At least one should make you smile!

01/21/24 10:45 pm.

V: Your guy is a bank robber? Why? Why?

F: He said the bank robbed him first. All of those fees.

V: You expect me to let a bank robber invest my money?

F: Who knows banks better than a bank robber….he did his research. Besides you know what Ben Franklin said.

V: What?

F: A fool and his money are soon parted.

V: Are you calling me a fool?

F: Let's' just say you didn't follow Ben Franklin's example.

V: What?

F: A penny saved is a penny earned….. You know he saved a penny a day, died with 10 thousand pennies, so the bank put his face on the 100 bill. The only bill you have with your face on it is your credit card bill. They wanted to know about your investments.

V: What investments?

F: …..good news bad news joke.

V: Are you trying to play me like a fool?

F: You know they made fun of old Ben Franklin too…the British did. They called him a Yankee Doodle.

V: I know, that was their insult to the early Americans. They made a song about it too.

F: Yeah, I know it. Let's sing it!

V: Are you trying to make me forget that you owe me money?

F: As Orville said to Wilbur, 'You're a Wright!'

(I'm trying to find a catch phrase that goes 'You're right!' but can't find one that works. The reference to the Wright Brothers is going to force me to go back into the routine and reference the Wright Brothers early on so that little joke will make sense in this spot.)

01/23/24

I'm juggling the jokes around in my head today. I think I'll end with the "Yankee Doodle" song, but then again a more unknown American Folksong from that period could work as well.

01/26/24

I like the stock joke about the diary…it made me smile….must use it in the routine.

F: Benny gave me the rules of being an investment banker. Rule one: If you use your own money, you're considered a genius and you're an entrepreneur.

V: And rule two….

F: Never use your own money…use other people's money!

V: And if you use other people's money?

F: Then you are a "broker"….and they are the "brokee."

V: What? I'm not going….

F: But don't worry, you're supposed to use your family's money first.

V: Good, glad to hear it.

F: Not so fast….my sister said she doesn't trust me with her money! She thinks I'll give it away along with her passwords. She doesn't think I respect her privacy.

V: Well it was nice of her to tell you that.

F: She didn't. I read it in her diary.

So if you can't get your family's money…use your friend's money. Hello Friend!

In reviewing some of the old stuff

V: Ben Franklin lived in 1776, the American Revolution.

F: Ben Franklin lives in 4F, the DuBois Apartments over on 10th Street.*

V: I'm talking about the year 1776….

01/27/24

Working on the ending joke….figure notes that I can't get money from this crowd of brokers or bankers….."They ain't lending, they're too happy!" Working on the wording……

I'm late! My normal cut-off for writing an assigned routine is 2 weeks. Two weeks to write followed by two weeks to rehearse for the Big Day. Since I said this is all REAL TIME I'm trying to follow my usual schedule…..BUT I got cut off tonight….I'm on a comic roll so the routine has to wait! I saw UNDERDOGS with Snoop Dog earlier. Then some show, SHERRI came on and that was it! I was on a roll! I'm going to share since it ties in to the important lessons in ventriloquism's comic dynamics. First UNDERDOGS…I laughed and I cried! Snoop can't act a lick! No matter what he's in…he's just SNOOP DOG and that's the appeal! Comedian Mike Epps was in the film. Mike Epps can't act a lick! He plays the same character no matter what movie he's in….and he steals the show every time! He's just Mike Epps…and that's why we fans love him! Understand that! I don't know that the French are correct with the thing about a "comic" flaw, but I know I'm a fan of Snoop and watch his offerings just because he's SNOOP. Mike Epps? Maybe I like his character because he comes across as THUG LIGHT!? In his films. Maybe? I just love to see his work. The late Jack Benny couldn't act outside of the character he created…the egotistical miser….loved by all! Larry David can't act outside of his character of the selfish prick….loved by all! Now take a moment and look at your figures and puppets. THEY MUST HAVE THAT! That is their "star power." Nina Conti's Monkey is Monkey always…that's why we love him! David Strausman's Ted E. Bear is always the same….that's why we love him! Jeff Dunham's Peanut is always insane….that's why we love him! ……..And now I can't think of any female figures… why is that?! Other than the late Wayland Flowers'

Madam…we have no female figures on the national stage? What! Somebody needs to fix that!……… My point is that your fans come back over and over to see your figures and puppets for their characters! If you do repeat engagements, please recognize this reality when putting together your sets. Don't disappoint with an all new cast….keep at least one of your strongest figures/puppets in your sets. Remember you and he/she are a comedy team.

Then there was Sherri…..this is clearly a show to take over Ellen Degeneris shows' demographic….women and gays. Sherri's a nice host, but that's why the show is lacking….too nice…she's a comedian. The show needs an edge…she needs to be a sarcastic comic like the late Joan Rivers or the great Wanda Sykes. As I'm watching the first 15 minutes of the show (before I turn it off), I'm reimagining Sherri as a more caustic comic and laughing like crazy as I create/correct the scenes and jokes. I'm mentioning this because these kinds of exercises keep your comic chops sharpened!

Reimagine shows…..what would you do if you or your figure hosted? It's a fun exercise. Try it!

****

The final script…..This is a first draft. As the date approaches I may add more to this script, but the basic script is complete. If I were really doing this piece, I would probably add a song….and may do so over the next section… maybe.

THE BANKING ROUTINE…..typed on 01/30/24 at 11:00 am. (see it in Part 3)

You have a set of jokes around your topic. You've put them into an order which you think will work for you and your figure/puppet. Now type it out so you have a script. If you have time, put it aside for a few days….you have another task.

THROW AWAYS... ADDING THE SPICE

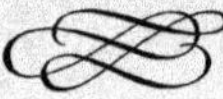

A Throw away joke is one that is performed, but is not emphasized during the set. These types of jokes add spice to your routine and keep the audience smiling. They can be visual but most of the time they are verbal. Rodney Dangerfield's throw away about his doctor is a classic. If you watch his work on YouTube, you'll find that he often comments on his own health…and in the course of it he mentions his doctor, Dr. Vinny Boom Ba. The doctor's name is a throw away joke. Sometimes in my show my puppets mention their favorite place, Pete's Pizza and Pastry Parlor in Poughkeepsie, Pennsylvania. It's a fun place name…shows my ventriloquist skill and gets a smile or two when one of us starts the name and the other finishes it. It's never emphasized, it's a throw away. I remember a Richard Pryer movie where a character was crushed and in the funeral scene, the coffin was thin (practically flat). Nothing was said about that, but it was hilarious....hence a throw away. The Monty Python troupe was brilliant at that kind of visual humor also.

Let's look for throw aways that you can use.....start with names. Keep reading your newspaper to find popular figures with unusual names you may be able to reference. A few months ago (in 2023) there were articles about then much maligned Senator Tommy Tupperville. He has an interesting name.....I can see my figure changing it to Senator Tommy Tupplewear.

****

F: I was so mad! It's summer! This "climate change thing" is getting me down. I wrote to my Congressman Tommy Tupplewear about it.

V: What happened?

F: I was walking down the street and suddenly whoosh!

V: Whoosh?

F: Whoosh! There was thunder. There was lightning! It was....rough! Then it started snowing. Snowing!

V: Snowing? That was hail!

F: You're telling me! I would have said that, but I thought this was a family show.

****

The use of comic names is old-school comedy. Phyliss Diller's husband "Fang" was a great comedy throw-away name back in the day, but it won't fly today. The current crop of stand-up comedians use their own situations to present "realistic" comedy, hence seemingly made-up comic names won't work anymore. WE ventriloquists have the advantage as our acts are "fantasy," hence throw-away fake names continue to delight our audiences. USE THEM!

In your joke file keep a list of comic names and places which you can reference when you are working on your routines. Comic foods are great too! If you see a name in the news that can bring a smile, make a note of it. Places, people, foods.... USE THEM! Again, you use them without emphasis and they add a punch to your routine.

A REVIEW OF THE WRITING PROCESS

You have chosen a topic.

You have focused on your topic by breaking it into categories of PEOPLE, PLACES/SPACES , THINGS AND WHATEVER.

You have written jokes for each category.

You have chosen the jokes that work best for you and your partner and placed them in a dialogue format.

You have placed the various dialogues in some type of order with a climax.

You have typed it out for rehearsal.

REHEARSING THE SCRIPT

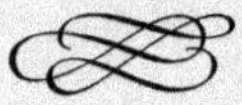

You have a typed script in hand. You're ready to start rehearsing. Practicing and rehearsal are two different processes. You practice in front of a mirror for lip control, enunciation and expression. You rehearse for the rhythm, comic timing and expression with your partner (your puppet or figure). Your rehearsal is no different than a rehearsal with a "real" person, so I'm writing this section assuming that you've had some experience in theater.

You must run through the script with your partner. No stopping. No laughing or breaking character…that's one of the main points of rehearsing with your partner. You must be able to go through the routine smoothly. You and your partner must respond to the dialogue appropriately but at the same time you must go for the laughs … .find the comic rhythm, know when to speed it up and slow it down (pacing) and most importantly how to relax and allow the audience to laugh. My accordion teacher once pointed out that when one plays alone, one plays slowly with expression. When one plays a piece for others, nervousness sets in and we students, rush through the piece without allowing others to enjoy it. Relaxing on stage is a must.

You don't need a mirror. With today's technology you can film your rehearsal on your cell phone. Be sure to have a notebook and make notes about it. This is especially important if you are a part-timer. These notes become very important and can be a life-saver when there is a gap of time between performances. The review of the rehearsal notes can swing you back into the rhythm of youhis r dialogue.

Real time: I'm beginning to dislike this book! I don't want to write something that I can't stand on….so I guess I'll take the next two weeks to rehearse and perform this BANK ROUTINE.

Looking at my calendar I'll usurp one of Son # 1's shows, he won't care. I'll have 10 days to get it ready for a senior center. I'll open for him. 15 minutes of his 60 minute set. I hope this dialogue is at least 10 minutes of rehearsal time sans laughs! Performance date: 02/09/24.

Notes:

Son # 1 has a higher paying gig so I'll now have to do the whole set. Great! 02/02/24

Rehearsals are going well….but the script seems too short. Will need to add a few more jokes. …".the stock going up and down seems okay," I chuckled.

SLOW DOWN! SLOW DOWN! 02/05/24

It's crunch time and I have to deal with Homeland Security? Really? 02/06/24

The script is fun, but it still seems too short….I'm thinking Ijangayanga needs to be Sidney Poitier …A Raisin In the Sun. (For those that don't know and haven't read his delightful autobiography…..he Stole the play from the main actress. The role of the mother was supposed to be The star role in this production. Poitier interpreted it differently and felt that the son Walter was the key player in the story. He upstaged the actress playing the mother As well as all the other actors. He never changed a word of the script. He did it through His cadence, his actions on stage and emphasis on various speeches. Ijangayanga needs to control his dialogue. Go slow. Use his eyes for gesturing. Wait when needed.

GO SLOW!

It's crunch time! 02/08/24

THE FIRST PERFORMANCE - An Adult Day Care Center

Not too bad. Small audience of about 25 seniors. The routine got a few chuckles and Laughs. I think I may have rushed it along….the problem in this case was that the format changed.

Originally, I was just going to introduce Son #1 with this routine, but he took another engagement. This left me with the entire one hour program. Thankfully my congo player was available to balance out the program. It's February (African-American History Month) and I just opened an experimental theater piece from east Africa for American audiences. Since I had no time to work on anything else, I decided to do my experimental piece there. Not a wise idea if one understands how to set up a performance- ventriloquist set. I have two more adult dates to perform this Banking Routine with my experimental piece…..so let me digress and write on what a "great" ventriloquist set should look like. This was definitely not one. "Experimental" theater pieces belong in your area's annual "Experimental Festival." In the Delaware Valley this is the FRINGE FESTIVAL and this merged piece would be a great fit for it. Traditional dance, storytelling with a drum and a puppet act together….perfect!

THE SECOND PERFORMANCE....... 02/16/24.....
A Rehab Center

Small Audience of about 20 - 25. A great set! This script has legs! Well, there's good news and bad news. The good news: Laughs galore!! The bad news.... unfortunately I couldn't finish the routine. I ran out of time. I (or I should say, "We") took our time. Ijangayanga was in top form and definitely milked the laughs. My vent act was not the main act, so we had only 8 - 10 minutes for the routine. I enjoyed it, but I felt bad afterwards as I dropped the ball on the ending. When I got the signal to end, I just kind of stopped and said good-bye to Ijangayanga and that was that. Here's one of my weaknesses as a comic, and definitely something I have to work on with my ventriloquist act....I can't pivot to the end joke. I really don't know how (yet). That last joke is the climax, but I don't know how to get there if I'm in the middle of a routine. I don't know how to pivot to a song either, so I just get stuck. I just stop and say good-bye. That kind of ending really sucks....I've got to work on "pivoting." One more set with the Banking Routine next week.....I'm going to keep rehearsing and working on it until then. ... the things I do for you, dear readers!

Notes:

02/19/24.....the script needs pruning. Some jokes seem a bit wordy. Cut them down to "perfect."

02/20/24…..I don't like the ending. It's not funny enough. Maybe it's the wording of that last line….

Maybe the whole concept of the two Benjamins isn't working. I need something better.

THE THIRD PERFORMANCE ……02/26/24…..A Senior Live-in Facility

This was a disaster! I'm sick with a slight virus. All of this from worry? Homeland Security…it never gets old! I never get sick. This is the first since….well, there was that POISON IVY last year, and that PINK EYE the year before….but never a virus not even during covid. I keep physically fit, healthy and take my vitamins….. but when I do fall under, my mind is gone. Something about those viruses that affects my mind. I'm like a "litunga" (a zombie). Thankfully the drummer was prepared to take control of the set. The vent moment started great…laughs galore…and then Kaput! I'm shooting blanks. My mind goes blank and I've got nothing. Benny who? I can't remember a thing. I switch to a standard set with Ijangayanga and let it lapse after a few minutes. Disaster! Sorry readers…..the script remains good, I just didn't get the final project done for you like I wanted. BUT LIFE IS LIFE!

I'll be performing this routine in other venues, but this is the final report for this book about it.

REVIEW AND LESSONS ON "THE BANK ROUTINE"

For the readers, I hope the process of creating a routine was made clear with the development of this one. I am pleased with the basic routine and will continue to develop and use it. Out of the three times noted that I performed it as a part of its development for this book, I got three more gigs from one of the sponsors.

FINDING YOUR NICHE...
UNDERSTANDING PLACES

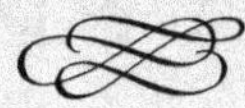

What works in one state/city may not work in another. Just be aware and go with the flow. It's one of those things that you learn on the road. You can't predict it….at least I don't think you can. Just listen to the laughs, shift the joke order around if need be. If the joke doesn't work in that area, drop it for that area. I'll never forget how the audience hated Son # 1 and my AMERICAN PORTRAITS show in Atlantic City. Yet this comedy was a major hit for the theater company and toured for at least two years with repeat engagements. What was with that Atlantic City crowd? Who knows. I got a return invitation ten years later…2023 to be precise…. A music festival. I declined. Son # 1 went and he bombed (again). He was forewarned…he should have listened…..kids!…. Know your places. Know your niches. If you're sure the venue is not one for you….decline the engagement. I don't do strip clubs or bars…..and no amount of money will entice me to go there just to bomb! I've been in bars to support my artist friends and for producer meetings….no thanks. I've never liked the crowd. You do have to be open if you are just getting started, so you will have to perform in spaces unknown. Go for it, but when you're done think about the space. Do you want to try it again? Do you want to tour it? Is that your niche? For me …clubs/ok; churches/ok; elementary schools/ok; community centers/ok; senior centers/ok; drug rehab centers/no; middle schools/no; high schools/sometimes; cruises/ sometimes if it's a day trip; outdoor fest/sometimes; outer space/Hmmm.

Some of my memorable performing venues…a migrant worker camp. I did the show during the day for their children. This was a very humbling experience for me and remains one of my show highlights. The children didn't speak much English so I didn't really think I was connecting. When the show was over there was silence followed by applause. As I'm packing the car the sponsor comes over and shakes my hand. She explained that the children were in awe and it was such a great show… that they were so overwhelmed that they couldn't clap for a while when I was done….and then! Wham…Applause. As I said, I was deeply humbled by the experience.

I fell out laughing when Jeff Dunham and Peanut did their bit about a show for a deaf audience. I've had the same experience! So I knew his was a real one! And lest I forget my shows in prisons....they are great audiences, but I don't look to do them often. The problem with prison shows is that the mates want friends on the outside...so they become penpals. You get letters! This would be okay if you have a personal secretary to answer them....but remember what I wrote about you, the performer living like Superman or Wonder Woman? You don't have time for casual friends! You can't have a penpal! They are an annoyance. Sorry. I remember one inmate got out and came over to visit....awkward! It was a short visit, but awkward! And speaking of letters, you will often get a stack from classes if you do school shows...one from each child! Again, if you don't have a secretary, letters from your fans can be a bit much to answer BUT answer you must! Generally I will write one thank you to the school, but if I have time I'll write one to each class from one of the puppets...it's just good manners.

ONE SECRET OF PERFORMING FOR CHILDREN

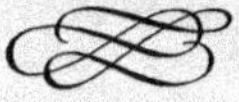

Since we're touching on spaces, let me share an important secret of performing for young audiences…..control the space. Children love puppets and (soft) figures. They also have a bit of fear of the puppets and figures as well….so they like to or need to touch the puppets just to make sure they are "not alive." If allowed, your young audience will mob you and the puppets, punch or hit the puppets or pull on the puppets just to see if they are alive. For this reason, you must have a good introduction to the puppets/figures of your show, but most importantly….YOU MUST CONTROL THE SPACE! You are the artist, your sponsor is not. Oftimes your sponsor will ask you to perform in "impossible" spaces, i.e. a space which will lead exactly to what I've just described. You must insist on what set ups you know will work. Birthday parties are difficult for this reason if you don't control the space. With children you need a "stage"....you need a safe "stage" for your puppets so you must have a line and a gap that the children must not cross. This has to be explained to the client AND you need an adult to enforce it. You can not enforce it, you are too busy with the show. If you have an assistant or producer, perhaps he or she can do it....but you are best served by someone from the venue whom the children are more likely familiar with. If you can not procure these two things, you can expect a rough time and not much of a show. Been there.

THE VENTRILOQUIST SET LIST

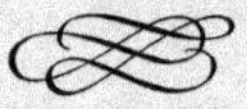

I believe what Senor Wences said about the number of puppets/figures being no more than 5. Personally, I limit it to 3 or 4 max to avoid stressing my voice. I try to start with a strong routine but not with my "strongest" comedy puppet/figure. It's kind of like a comedy club….the headliner goes last. So put your strongest partner and his/her routine last. Put your newest routine in the middle of the set sandwiched between the more established routines/figures. Thus in a good set that BANKING ROUTINE would be the second routine not the first. It's still new to me…I'm still working on it so I don't want to start with it…I want to establish my comedy and style with the audience first.

If the BANKING ROUTINE fails, I still have a powerhouse routine and figure waiting. Actually after the newest routine in the center, I would perform a bit of magic or give my drummer a slot before ending with my headliner partner. The structure of your set is important. It needs to climax with your best.

THE SET: 45 minutes - 1 hour

STRONG INTRODUCTION WITH FIGURE #1

NEWEST ROUTINE WITH FIGURE/PUPPET # 2

MAGIC OR MUSICAL NOVELTY

THE HEADLINER : PUPPET/FIGURE # 3

PART III
A SAMPLE OF MY ROUTINES

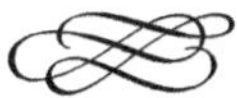

These routines are not "literary" pieces; they are dynamic. If you ever hear me perform them, you will find that they may not follow the exact order, as I change them to match the audience. I also alter them to fit my moods and update them as I add new jokes. That is how your routines should be viewed: constantly upgrading and improving as you rehearse and perform them.

ADULT ROUTINE

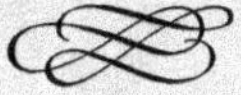

<u>THE CLUB</u>

(NANDI THE RABBIT = N./ KI = VENTRILOQUIST)

N: Let's hurry this up, Kiwi, I have somewhere important to go.

K: You didn't tell me that. Where?

N: I've got a club meeting to be at. I'm running for president of my new club.

K: You're in a club? You never mentioned that! What's it called? I'm all ears!

N: That's it exactly!

K: It's called, 'That's it exactly?'

N: No, no.

K: Well what is it?? I'm all ears!

N: Exactly!

K: It's called exactly?

N: No, it's called, 'I'm all ears!'

K: 'I'm all ears!?' What kind of club is it? What do you do at this club?

N: We talk about everybody! We talk about everybody we like....

K: Uh-huh.

N:...and everybody we don't like...

K: Uh-huh.

N:...and everybody in between.....we talk about everybody!

K: So it's a club of gossiping.

N: We don't call it gossiping...it's more like a live twitterfeed. It's facebook live! We're all ears!

K: How many rabbits are in this club? What's the attendance like?

N: Our attendance is 100%.

K: 100%?

N: Yes, 'cause if you miss a meeting, we're gonna talk about you! We're all ears!

K: Men don't like gossiping! Is this a co-ed club?

N: Well it used to be...but then every time there was a meeting, we'd have a population explosion --- AND more to talk about! So the men formed their own club.

K: What's that called? We're all ears Too?

N: No, no not ears! But I can't say...this is a family show! We're all ears!

K: I'm curious...what did you talk about at your last meeting?

N: Oh, we talked about you.

K: Me?

N: Yeah, remember you and your girlfriend broke up. You had that argument....

K: Thank you! Enough! How did you even find out about that?!

N: We're all ears!

K: Where do you hold these meetings?

N: It's just a little hole-in-the-wall.

K: That's not a nice thing to say about someone's place.

N: No, it really is a 'hole-in-the-wall' over on
_______________ street. We all get together
there...sing a few songs, talk, have a few drinks.

K: Drinks!? Rabbits drink??

N: Have you ever tried celery juice straight? Yuck! It needs
a shot of vodka!

N: But I really need to go now. I've got to get to my
meeting. I'm running for president.

K: I could help you with that. I know a little about
campaigns. Why my cousin was a campaign manager of a
major political party.

N: Oh yes, that's the cousin that got arrested for accepting
a bribe...got four years for that.

K: Hey! How did you know that?

N: We're all ears!

K: Nonetheless, I could be your campaign manager. I
could help everyone know what you stand for.

N: No, I need someone who's going to confuse everyone.

K: What?

N: Don't you know politics? You only get elected if you
confuse everyone..make outrageous claims, make promises
you can't keep...use statistics nobody understands.

K: Now that shows you don't understand politics. You want to run on a solid platform...appeal to the will and desires of the people ...reach into the dept of their souls to elevate them to reach the heights of their aspirations!

N: Wow...are you confusing! You're hired!

K: Thank you. Now let's start with what you believe in. What do you believe in...

N: I believe in anything that will get me elected!

K: What if it's unethical, unsavory, even unjust?

N: And you'd rather it be?

K: Ethical, just and...and...savory?

N: Now you're being unjust! Never mention 'savory' and 'rabbit' in one sentence!

Let's stick with unsavory, unjust and unethical!

K: That just spells dishonesty. Why I would never vote for that! I would never ever vote for a dishonest person!

N: Then you're fired!

K: What? Why?

N: You've never ever voted!

THE DOG ROUTINE: MY HOBBY

D: Hey Mr. Kiwi did you say hobby? Say no more, I've got a good one….

K: You? You've got a hobby?

D: Yes I do! Yes, I do! Yes, I do!

K: I didn't know dogs would know anything about hobbies.

D: Why, what do you think we do all day…walk, eat and sleep?

K: That's all I ever see you do.

D: That's because you're a day person and I'm a night dog. You sleep while I eat. Now guess what my hobby is?

K : Sleeping, eating or walking?

D: No, no and no. I'll give you a hint. What do Rembrandt, Piccasso and Bozo the clown Have in common?

K: Rembrandt and Picasso were painters….Bozo?

D: They were all painters.

K: Bozo? Bozo the clown, a painter?

D: He paints his face.

K: So you're a painter?

D: Yes I am. Yes, I am. Yes, I am.

K: Well what medium do you use? What's your medium?

D: Oh no, I'm not a medium, I'm a large.

K: I'm talking about your paint. You know some of them are poison.

D: Don't worry about me. I'm a safe painter, I paint with food.

K: Food?

D: Yes, just yesterday I was painting with tomato soup.

K: Do you have a teacher?

D: Yes, but she doesn't think I know my colors.

K: Dogs are color blind. Do you know your colors?

D: Do I know my colors? Do I know my colors? Do I know my colors?

K: Well do you?

D: Not really. I know vanilla, chocolate and strawberry.

K: I see what your teacher means…

D: Do you want to see my work. I've got some here…..right over there.

K: (takes out one with nothing on it) I think I just took a blank paper.

D: No, that's one of my pictures. Look carefully.

K: I don't see anything. What is it?

D: That is a painting of a cow eating grass.

K: Where's the grass?

D: The cow ate it.

K: Where's the cow?

D: Mr. _____, you don't think the cow's gonna stick around after she ate the grass. Do you?

K: One down. I see what your teacher sees.

D: I've got another one over there. Look at that one, it's for sale.

K: (takes out another blank picture) ....and what is this? Another cow eating grass?

D: No, no....look carefully, look carefully....

K: I'm looking, I don't see anything. What is it?

D: That is a snowman in a snowstorm.

K: Great.

D: You'll really like the next one. My teacher loved it!

K: (takes out another blank) Don't tell me...a snow-woman in a snow storm?

D: No. Look carefully....look carefully.

K: I give up, what is it?

D: That is a white car in a foamy car wash.

K: That's it! I'm done!

D: My teacher said I could be in the Guiness Book of World Records.

K: The Guiness Book of World Records for what?

D: The most useless paintings.

K: That's something I can see. Now moving on....

D: Wait, you don't want to miss the next one....it's a portrait.

K: A portrait?

D: Yes, a portrait of you!

K: (takes out picture with a colored triangle) A portrait? Is this an abstract?

D: No.

K: Modern?

D: No.

K: New tech?

D: No.

K: How is this a portrait of me? Where am I? This is just a triangle.

D: That's your nose.

K: My nose?

D: Yes, it's so big….I couldn't get anything else on there.

K: I give up! What made you think you could be an artist? Why painting as a hobby?

D: I wanted to find my roots. I wanted to know who am I and where did I come from.

K: If you wanted to know your roots, why didn't you just go to the kennel?

D: They don't like me over there at that kennel.

K: Oh, I forgot! You peed all over their floor.

D: That's because that big dog barked at me!

K: That wasn't a big dog, that was the owner.

D: She was big! She made you pee a little too didn't she.

K: So exactly how did you find this hobby?

D: I called a psychic hotline.

K: Kit, don't you know those psychic hotlines are big ripoffs. I hope you didn't lose too Much money.

D: Oh I didn't. It didn't cost me a cent.

K: Good.

D: I used your credit card. She told me all about my past life.

K: Reincarnation?

D: No, Ms. Rihanna….psychic to the stars.

K: You're a star?

D: No, I'm related to a famous painter……Reinheimer Himerdingle.

K: Reinheimer Himerdingle?

D: Yes, he's a famous painter. He's in the Guiness Book of World Records.

K: And you're related to him?

D: According to Ms. Rihanna.

K: I admit, I've never heard of him. Do you have your phone? Mine is on my charger.

D: Yes, it's right over there.

(K takes the phone)

K: I'll just ask Alexa.

D: I don't have Alexa, I've got her cousin Tamika….Alexa was a little expensive and she asked too many questions about your credit card.

K: Tamika huh? (talks to Tamika….she answers with your telephone voice)

Tamika? Who is …….

T: Is that how you greet somebody? Just start barking orders?

K: Sorry. How are you Tamika?

T: I could be better if folks would stop asking dumb questions. Now what's yours?

K: Have you ever heard of Reinheimer Himerdingle?

T: Reinheimer Himerdingle? The famous painter? He's in the Guiness Book of World Records.

K: Who is he?

T: He's a house painter. He lives in Ugo Utah.

K: A house painter?

T: Yes, he's in the Guiness Book of World Records for having painted the most houses In a single city.

K: The most houses?

T: Yes. A world record….The most houses…..

K: Where?

T: Ugo Utah. Population …..six.

CHILDREN'S BIRTHDAY PARTY

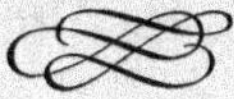

(4 animal puppets….tote change bag, sucker coin box, 20th century silks)

The ventriloquist's interaction with the puppets is scripted. The puppet interaction with the children is ad-libbed. The goal is to interact with every single child in the course of the show.

The show is ad-libbed so one has to know one's puppets well to succeed at it. One also must be good at reading a room and at managing a party of children.

Note: if you don't like children, forget about it! It's one of those jobs that you can't do for money alone! AND if you are picky about your props and puppets….forget about it! Take only your inexpensive props and "touchable" puppets, i.e. do not take your $ 200. Silk cascade or your $ 1000. Figure….they will be touched by someone in the course of the party…when you least expect it! I make my own spring flowers, so I didn't get mad when I produced them….experienced an audible "OOOO" by the children and they all ran up and took them away! Let's not talk about Kit, the dog! Children everywhere love to run up and pull his ears….I have no idea why! Managing these situations is essential!

My puppets are a turtle, a dog, a rabbit and a (snake) dragon

A. Comedy Introduction: If you don't know any, read a few David Ginn Books.

B. (The Turtle)

V: And now I'd like to sing "HAPPY BIRTHDAY" to ___________________. Let me take

Out my piano….(takes and opens bag)

T: Trick or Treat! (still in bag)

V: Amina! What are you doing here?

T: Me here for 'Trick or Treat.'

V: Well come on out and say "hello" to everyone. (out of bag, but now inside shell)

T: No, no, no. Me scared.

V: You don't have to be afraid…these are nice people.

T: Are they smiling?

V: Everybody smile!....Yes, they are smiling. Come on out.

T: No, no, no. Are they clapping their hands?

V: Everybody clap….they're clapping…come on out.

T: Me take peek. (peers out of shell) Okay, they look okay. (now out) Trick or Treat!

V: Amina, it's not time for 'Trick or Treat,' it's a birthday party.

T: Me no have birthday party today…it's 'Trick or Treat' day, me want candy.

V: No, it's not your birthday, it's _______________________'s birthday.

T: Who? Who's _______________________? (begins addressing various children)

Are you _______________________? Are you _______________________? Are you

_______________________? (reacts to each response) Who's _______________________?

(when she meets the birthday child)...Trick or Treat! Me want candy!

V: That's _______________________. It's his/her birthday.

T: Treat! Treat! Treat!

V: This is where you sing "Happy Birthday."

T: (to birthday child) Do you like me costume?

V: Wait a minute. You're not wearing a costume.

T: Yes, I am. Me "Invisible Girl."

V: The "Invisible Girl" from the Fantastic Four?

T: Yes.

V: Well, where is this costume?

T: It's invisible! And now me sing " Happy Birthday." (to birthday child) Me sing to

You. (starts clearing throat over and over. Then a series of "Do-Ra-Mi" and

"Mi-Mi-Mi")

V: Are you ready?

T: Me ready. (Opens and closes mouth as if singing the birthday song.)

V: What are you doing?

T: Me singing. (continues opening and closing mouth as if singing.)

V: We can't hear anything!

T: That's because me using me "invisible voice!"

Trick or Treat!

V: Thank you Amina. We've heard enough! Let's thank Amina for coming out!

Everybody, clap your hands! Good-bye Amina.

(places Amina away. Takes out next bag.)

****

V: This is a good spot to sing "Happy Birthday!" Let me take out my drum.

(Opens bag.) Kit! Kit, what are you doing in there!

(Kit the dog appears)

K: Hey, ______________. I'm so excited! I've got a new hobby!

V: Everyone, here's my friend Kit, the dog.

K: Hey everybody! You're just in time to see my new hobby!

V: What is your new hobby?

K: I'm doing magic now. I'm a magician!

V: A magician?

K: Yes, I'm the Amazing Dogini! (bows) Hey, they're not clapping. Clap please!

V: Everybody, clap….

K: Thank you. I'm Dogini!

V: Well, you're just in time. We're at a birthday party. Maybe you can do some magic.

K: A birthday party! Say no more….I can use my magic to see just who's having a Birthday. I can look into the eyes and know just who's who….who's birthday and how old. Let me see…..Aha! It's your birthday! (starts picking children at random. Tries to find the birthday child, but fails as he speaks to each)…..

(Finally gives up….) Whose birthday is it? (the children point out the birthday child) Oh! I knew it! I knew it! Happy Birthday! Would you like to see some magic? ……

K: Who likes magic? ……..I, the Amazing Dogini will now do some! If you want to see magic, stand up! Stand up! (the children stand)

V: Wait a minute….you don't stand to see magic. Everybody sit down! Sit down!

(They sit)

K: I'm Dogini! I know what I'm doing! If you want to see magic, stand up! Stand up!

(the children stand)

V: What are you doing? You don't stand up to do magic! Everybody sit down! Sit Down! (the children sit)

K: I know what I'm doing! Stand up! Stand up! (to Vent) You too!

V: Alright, everybody stand up!

K: Okay now, to do magic….jump up and down five times…..(the children do each)

Turn around four times……..touch your nose three times….sit down two times…..

V: This is magic?

K: No, this is (morning/afternoon/evening) exercise….we didn't get to the magic yet.

V: Very funny. Everybody sit back down. Now where's the magic?

K: I'm going to make a dog biscuit disappear.

V: A dog biscuit?

K: Who wants to see a dog biscuit disappear? (answers from children)

V: Wait a minute….I don't want to see a dog biscuit disappear. I know what You're going to do. Your going to show us a dog biscuit and then you're Going to eat it to make it disappear. I know that trick!

K: Okay you got me….but I was going to put it into a box first. Do you have

A coin?

V: Yes, I do….right here…(takes out a large coin)

K: How about I teach you how to make it disappear?

V: Me? I'm going to do magic?

K: I'm going to teach you. Get my box over there.

(takes out the Sucker Coin Box)

K: Now this is a secret….everyone cover your ears! This is a secret…

(some children will, most won't so Kit tries to get them to do so…)

V: Just tell me what to do…..

(Kit whispers in his ear…)

You want me to tilt it?

K: Sshhh….it's a secret!

V: Oh right…are you sure this will work?

K: If it doesn't work, you'll need everyone to do real magic! Everyone, if this doesn't work just say the magic word together.

V: Say the magic word together….

K: Yes, together.

V: Okay, so what's the magic word we have to say?

K: Everybody, what's the magic word? (answers…..) No, no, no! The magic word is "together!"

V: Are you sure?

K: I'll check my magic book…..(Kit goes into his bag)

V: I'm just going to start…..

(The Sucker Coin Box Vanish is presented. After exposing his failure to vanish the coin, he asks everyone to say a magic word….someone will say that they should try "Abracadabra." He has them all say it together….both doors are opened. The coin has vanished.)

It worked! Thank you Kit. Let's thank him for his magic trick….. (applause)

(If I need a long show, here is where I now perform the 20th century silk illusion. …this is the spot for another magic routine, not a short trick, but a routine which can run 5 - 10 minutes)

****

(Puts the box away……voice comes from another small bag….)

Voice in bag: Terrible! Terrible! Terrible!

V: (takes out bag and looks in) Nandi! What are you doing here!

R: Terrible! Terrible! Terrible!

V: Everyone, it's my friend Nandi the Rabbit!

R: (comes out) This is terrible! Terrible! Terrible! Terrible!

V: What? What's terrible?

R: It's a birthday party....and you haven't sung happy birthday yet!

Terrible! Terrible! Terrible!

Hello everyone! I've been listening. I can't believe you haven't sung yet!

But I'm here now, so I'll do it! I will sing 'Happy Birthday.' Whose birthday is it? (to the birthday child) Happy Birthday! You look great for your age! (Names an Age which is older......and is corrected.) You mean you're _________? Are you sure? (to all) I will now sing 'Happy Birthday!'

(clears throat. Does voice exercises....clears throat again)

V: Are you going to sing?

R: Quiet! I'm going to sing.......

(begins a series of songs....none of which are Happy Birthday.)

V: Since you're not sure of the song, why don't you count to three and we'll all Sing together..

R: Okay….we'll all sing together when I count to three….

One….five…..seven….four….twelve…..

V: Is that how you count to three?

R: Yes.

V: Everyone, how do we count to three…. (they count)

R: Oh, the shortcut! I've got it! One……………..Two………………..three.

(they sing)

R: Now it's time for lettuce and carrots! Let's eat!

V: We don't have lettuce and carrots for birthdays. What do we have, everyone?

(they answer)

R: I'll wait for my carrots! Good-bye!

(puts her back in the bag)

****

V: Speaking of ice-cream and cake, I brought some cupcakes along for the party. Where are they……(takes out the box with the dragon-snake) (looks into the box, then shuts it quickly) It's Ijangayanga! He's a baby dragon. Oh Ijangayanga!

Ij: Hey, _____. Hey everybody.

V: Ijangayanga, did you see some cupcakes in this box?

Ij: Cupcakes?

V: Yes, cupcakes….you know, little cakes about this big…

Ij: Did they have vanilla and strawberry icing?

V: Yes, that's them.

Ij: No, haven't seen them.

V: That's funny, they were in this box.

Ij: Hold on, let me see if they're around…(dips into box and starts throwing all kinds of paper balls out)….

V: Stop! You're making a mess!

Ij: That wasn't me….that was them! You folks are messy! This is one messy party!

(the children respond)

V: Ijangayanga, you need to clean up your mess.

Ij: Okay already! (to individual children) Could you help me? Could you pick that up? (to V) Now are you happy?

V: I would be if I had something to share with everyone. You ate my cupcakes!

Ij: Would you like me to make something that you can share? I am a dragon, I do know magic.

V: You can make something? Cupcakes?

Ij: Well no...I'm not that good at magic yet. But I can make some things....

In fact I know something that I could give everyone, especially________ (the birthday child). It's small. It's light and it's something everybody can use. It's the perfect present! Wait, I have some right here I can share! And now everybody, here's a present from __________. (goes into box and begins throwing out pieces of something "invisible" addressing various children as he does so....) Here's a little for you....and you. Here's a big piece for you...and you.

V: Wait a minute! What is this? What are you sharing?

Ij: It's AIR! Everybody needs AIR!

V: I don't want AIR! I want something better for a birthday party...a perfect Present.

Ij: Do you still have that magic bag? How about I say a magic word and make (the birthday child) a nice pet? Everybody loves a pet.

V: Now that sounds nice....

Ij: Okay, ____________. Would you like a shark? Everybody likes sharks….they're pets, aren't they? No? Okay, how about a T-Rex. There's nothing like a T-Rex for a pet, right?

V: Let's just make something small…..

Ij: Okay, worms it is! Just take the bag, wave your hand and everyone say 'HAPPY BIRTHDAY!' Try it! (Ijangayanga goes back into the box)

V: (takes up the bag) Let's try it….maybe they'll be gummy worms.

(hand is waved. Everyone says the magic word. BALLOONS are produced from the bag.)

V: BALLOONS! That is a perfect present. Let's thank Ijangayanga by clapping and saying 'thank you!' (they do it as Ijangayanga's box is put away along with all the other puppets) Now who wants a balloon animal? Make a line behind ________(the birthday child)

(as they are lining up, you pack everything away so you're ready to leave once the animals are finished.)

****

CHRISTIAN FELLOWSHIP

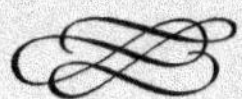

V= vent; T = Turtle; D = Dog; R = Rabbit)

V: Hello everyone. It's nice to be here today.

T: (in bag) Hello. Hello. Is anyone out there?

V: Amina? Is that you? Come on out and say hello.

T: (peeks out) Who's here today? I'm here to evangelize. Do you like my hat?

V: It's a very nice hat. You're here to evangelize? I didn't know you are an evangelist.

T: Oh yes, me evangelist everywhere. Do you?

V: Well no.

T: Me see why…you no have hat. Do you like me hat? It's my evangelist hat. Me wear everywhere.

V: How long have you been an evangelist?

T: Ever since me get hat.

V: I see….how much training did you get to be an Evangelist?

T: No training, me get hat.

V: A hat? Is that all you need to be an evangelist? What about a Bible?

T: Bible? What's that?

V: The book you need to teach God's word.

T: Oh is that what it's called? Me have one too. Me carry it around.

V: To be an evangelist, don't you have to open it and teach from it?

T: No. Me have hat. Everyone likes me hat. Do you like me hat?

V: Being an evangelist is not about hats, you have to teach from the Bible. You know, God's word, the Ten Commandments, the parables….do you know those.

T: Me no know.

V: You need to know a little. Let's take a parable from Jesus.

T: What is parable?

V: A story from Jesus is a parable.

T: If you no like it, don't tell it.

V: No, a parable is a story with cymbals.

T: Me hear parable yesterday…the Boston Symphony parable.

V: Let me tell you one of the parables…the parable of the talents.

T: Me no have time, must evangelize. Don't you see hat?

V: Well, how do you reach people as an evangelist?

T: Me start by singing.

V: Singing? You sing about Jesus?

T: Yes, me sing. Would you like to hear a song?

V: Okay. Let's hear one of your evangelist songs.

T: I wrote this one myself. It one of me favorites….(clears throat)

V: Well….

T: (clears throat)

V: Well….

T: Me get ready…..

(starts singing). LA! LA! LA! LA! LA! LA! LA! LA! LA! LA! LA! LA!

V: Excuse me….

T: Me no finished…..LA! LA! LA! LA! LA! LA! LA! LA! LA! LA! LA! LA! LLLAAAAA!

V: Does this song have Jesus in it?

T: Yes, it's coming…..LA! LA! LA! LA! LA! LA! LAAA!

V: Where's "Jesus?"

T: He coming at the end……LA! LA! LA! LA! LAAA! LA! LA! LA! LA! LA! LA! LA! LA! ….JESUS!

V: What kind of evangelizing is that?

T: It's perfect when you wear a hat. Do you like my hat? Me go now to do some more evangelizing.

V: Now wait a minute. Being an evangelist is not about singing. It's about telling everyone how Jesus changed your life….how you fell down and Jesus lifted you up. That's what we want to hear…how you fell down and Jesus lifted you up.

T: Oh you dumb.

V: Dumb?

T: Yeah….he dumb. Jesus can't lift me up….Me

Turtle. Me no can fall. Turtles no fall. We low to ground.

V: We'll, how did you find Jesus.

T: Me find Jesus in water.

V: You mean in baptism?

T: No…in ocean. One day me swimming along…in ocean nice and slow…LA. LA LA!

V: Swimming along…

T: …and me see jellyfish….

V: Jellyfish? Oh they're dangerous.

T: Me know….it swim right past me….then me see barricuda!

V: Barricuda….oh they're dangerous!

T: Me know….it swim right past me….then me see alligator.

V: An alligator! Those are dangerous! I guess you thanked the Lord for protecting you.

T: No…then me see what making them all swim….me see shark! Then me scream, "Jesus!" And me start swimming!!…me past them all! So, Jesus didn't pick me up when me fall…he pick me up when me slow! Just call on Jesus; He'll carry you through the water!(Placed back in bag)

****

V: That was interesting…..

(voice from another bag: "Is Nandi out there?")

V: Who? (looks into bag) Kit, is that you?

D: I think so. Is Nandi (the rabbit) out there?

V: No.

D: Good, we're not speaking. (Comes out)

V: Everyone this is _______, the dog.

D: Hey everybody! I just…..Mr. _________ there's a bee flying over your head! Look out!

V: (starts ducking) Where? Where?

D: (starts laughing) I got you! I got you!

V: So it was just a trick?

D: Yeah! I got you!

V: Very funny. So what's going on between you and________ the rabbit?

D: We're not friends anymore. She found herself a "new" friend.

V: You've met this friend…and you don't like him or her?

D: Never met…. This friend has changed her though. She doesn't like to play tricks on anyone anymore. ….and I love tricks! Look out! There's another bee flying over your head!

V: (waving hand around) Where? Where?

D: (laughing) I got you again! Boy, are you dumb!

V: Hey! No wonder _________ doesn't want to be friends anymore! Stop playing tricks!

D: Now you sound like her! According to her, her friend tells her not to trick anyone anymore. What kind of fun is that? Her friend doesn't want her to do anything! Hey you (pointing out someone in the audience)! There's a bumbly bee over your head! I got you!

V: I can see why. I think I'd like to meet this friend.

D: We'll you can't. _________ can't even pronounce his name. It's Spanish, and she can't even say it. It's pronounced "Hesus!" She says it's "Jesus." Can you believe that?

V: Jesus! He's the best friend that you can have!

D: Don't tell me, he's your friend too!

V: He's been my friend a long time…since I was a little lad.

D: So he's an old man! I'm going to tell _______'s mom!

V: What are you going to tell her…that Jesus is the Son of God and that he's been around a long time! He's there for everyone. He helps you when you're in trouble; he helps you know right and wrong. He's a great friend! You should try him out!

D: Where does he hang out? At the donut shop?

V: No. You can learn about Jesus in Sunday School.

D: School? No thanks. I had enough school already. I'm finished with school.

V: You mean you graduated?

D: No. I just stopped going…I'm finished with school.

V: How many years did you go?

D: Years? No, no, no.

V: No? How many months did you go?

D: Months? No, no, no.

V: How many weeks did you go?

D: Weeks?

V: How many days did you go?

D: One. `

V: One?

D: Yeah, one. You can learn a lot in one day.

V: What did you learn in that one day?

D: I learned I didn't like school.

V: Well, Sunday school is not like regular school. It's only one day and usually only an hour.

D: An hour? Count me in!

V: Good. You can learn about Jesus.

D: That guy again! Count me out!

V: It's a good place to learn the parables....

D: What's a parable.

V: It's a short story that Jesus tells that has a lesson. It's a parable.

D: We'll, if you don't like it, don't tell it!

V: Parables are great! Let's look at the parable of the talents.

D: Talents? And what is a talent?

V: There was a time when a talent was a form of money. Today, a talent is a skill....something somebody can do? Everybody has one.

D: You have one? What's your talent?

V: I'm a ventriloquist. I can throw my voice.

D: Well why don't you throw it on out of here along with yourself.

V: No thanks. I'm going to tell you the parable of the talents. A long time a go there was a one who had three servants. One day he called his servants in front of him and said, 'I'm going off, take care of the place. And to each he gave some talents. To the first servant he gave 7 talents.

D: Seven? So many?

V: Yes, seven. To the second, he gave three.

D: Only three?

V: Yes, three. And to the third servant he gave one talent.

D: One?

V: Yes, one.

D: Must have been the ventriloquist in the group!

V: And then the master went away. Well those servants started thinking about those talents. The first servant took his seven talents and invested them ... .then after five years, he came up with seven more talents. The servant with the three, he invested them as well and he came up with three more talents. But the servant with the one, he was afraid to invest his, so he hid it. He buried his talent.

D: Buried?

V: Yes, buried.

D: Goes to show you can never trust a ventriloquist.

V: After five years the master returned. He called all of his servants to him and asked about the talents. The first servant said, "Master, you gave me seven talents and I took them out and made seven more." The Master said, "Thou good and faithful servant, you may enter the gates of heaven."

D: Heaven? Okay.

V: Then the second servant said, "Master, you gave me three talents, and I went out and got three more." And the Master said, " Oh good and faithful servant, you may enter the gates of heaven."

D: And the last servant? The ventriloquist with the one talent?

V: The servant with the one said, "Master, I know that you can be mad sometimes, so I didn't want you to be mad, so I buried my talent….but here it is.

D: He should have thrown his voice around now.

V: And the Master got mad. He said, "Thou wicked and slothful servant, I gave you one and you wasted it! Enter thou into the gates of darkness!"

D: Sad! Sad! Sad!

V: And you know what the lesson is in this parable of Jesus?

D: Yeah, don't be a ventriloquist…..they got no talent.

V: No! We should use everything that we have for the glory and honor of God! Now what do you have that you can use?

D: I don't know....what do I have? My eyes...my ears....my nose...my throat?

V: You're reminding me of a song...."tout au fond." It's an old French song.....

D: Well, find an old French person and sing it to them. I'll sing something else.

V: Okay. We'll keep it simple....let's sing "＿＿＿＿＿＿＿＿＿＿＿＿＿＿"

D: Okay.

(they end with a simple gospel song.)

KWANZAA

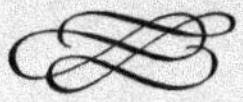

(Kwanzaa is an African-American December holiday. This routine can be adapted to just about any December holiday as there are so many similarities and the routine doesn't focus on specifics.)

(Ki -K and Amina, the Turtle -T)

K: And now I'd like……

T: Be quiet up there! Me trying to sleep down here!

K. What?

T: I said me trying to sleep down here!

K: Who is that (taking out bag. Removes Amina)? Amina? Amina come on out…

T: Me sleeping (snores)

K: It's Kwanzaa!

T: Again? We did it yesterday!

K: Yesterday? Come on out! (takes her out) Everybody, this is Amina… Amina, it's Kwanzaa, what do you say to everybody?

T: Oh you should have been at that Kwanzaa yesterday! It was so fun! We was dancing! We was singing! Me was rapping! It was ----

K: Excuse me?

T: My house was rocking! Even Kenji the lion was singing...and you know he no sing! Me was rapping! Even Nandi was there...she knocked over the ice-cream and we was skating...

K: You had Kwanzaa at your house?

T: Yeah, me house last night. OOO! Me house was rocking! Nandi started dancing and she knocked over the ice cream…

K: No one told me about it!

T: I know…..she knocked over the ice-cream and we was...

K: No one told me about it!

T: I know….

K: No one told me about it!

T: I know!!….you weren't invited!!

K: What? You didn't invite me to Kwanzaa? I'm the one that told you about Kwanzaa first. "I!" Me! Me! Me!

T: There's no no "I" in Kwanzaa, and there's no "you" in it either. You "stay" home.

K: What?

T: You stay home.

K: Why wasn't I invited? Do you know what Kwanzaa means?

T: Kwanzaa means first fruits….nothing to do with you.

K: It's got UMOJA in it. Umoja - Unity…to strive for and maintain unity in the family, community, nation and race. Not inviting me…was that "unity?"

T: Yes, it was. We animals got "together" and we all agreed…"together"….you not invited.

K: Why? Why wasn't I invited?

T: Well…

K: Is it because you animals don't like my singing "Everywhere I Go, everybody's talking About Kwanzaa?"

T: Well…

K: Is it because every year I have to get on you animals about how to put up the Kwanzaa things…

T: Well…

K: Is it because you get tired of my making you guys sing the Nguzo Saba song, which you think is too long…which by the way goes all the way back to 1966 when Kwanzaa began!

T: Well …… those good reasons…me use those next year.

K: Why wasn't I invited?

T: You really want to know? That gonna cost you.

K: Cost? I have to pay to find our why?

T: Yeah, first fruits cost money.

K: How much?

T: Ninety-nine dollars and ninety-nine cents.

K: Ninety-nine dollars!

T: …and ninety-nine cents!

K: I don't have ninety-nine dollars….I have a ten…

T: Me take. (takes it) Don't forget you owe me.

K: Just tell me why. Why wasn't I invited?

T: You weren't invited because my Kwanzaa was at my summer house….

K: Summer house? Where's that?

T: Underwater….in the ocean! You can't go there…you'd drown. Bye!

K: Hey!

MY SCHOOL PARTY

(WITH Ki (K) and Kit the Dog (D)

D: Mr. Kiwi, is that you?

K: Yes, it is. Kit? Kit, is that you?

D: It might be…let me see…I think it's me….(appears) I think it's me…of course I could be somebody else.

K: Everyone, this is Kit the dog.

D: Or I could be somebody else, I'm not sure.

K: Well, Kit, is there something you'd like to say to us.

D: No, no, no, I don't think so.

K: Look around…what do you see.

D: (sees Kinara) Oh, it's a birthday! (starts singing) Happy Birthday to you!….Whose birthday is it?

K: It's nobody's birthday.

D: Happy Birthday Dear Nobody!

K: No, I'm sure it's somebody's birthday…..

D: Happy Birthday Dear Somebody!

K: ….but we're not celebrating it!

D: What? You're not very nice. It's somebody's birthday and you're not celebrating it…you're cranky today.

K: I'm not cranky.

D: Don't you know it's Kwanzaa. It's time to celebrate "Umoja"…that means unity. You should have been at yesterday's Kwanzaa ceremony at my school!

K: I wasn't invited.

D: Well I can see why….you're cranky! You talk about celebrating somebody's birthday, then you take it back.

K: Just a minute, was this Kwanzaa ceremony under the ocean….

D: Yes it was, my school is at Amina's summer house.

K: You go to school underwater? In the ocean?

D: Yep! I'm in a school of fish! I put on my Scooby Dooby stuff and then I jump into the ocean. Yep! I'm Scooby Dooby. They say I'm a dog fish.

It was quite a party…I did some of my famous knock-knock jokes there…

K: Knock knock jokes?

D: Yeah, knock, knock.

K: Can you knock underwater?

D: Knock, knock!

K: Who's there?

D: Zawa…

K: Zawa? Zawa who?????????

D: Zawadi.

K: Zawadi. Zawadi? I didn't get it.

D: Neither did I….so make sure you bring it tonight! (laughs)

K: Very funny. So, while you're here you can help me to sing my favorite Kwanzaa song, 'everywhere I go, Everybody's talking about Kwanzaa.'

D: Oh wait! I hear my auntie calling me.

K: Your auntie?

D: Yeah.

K: I don't hear anything…

D: That's because it's very faint. I'm coming auntie!

K: Your aunt lives in Canada! I don't think you hear anything….I think you're trying to get out of singing with me….

D: Wow! (to audience) He's smart! Bye!

IJANGAYANGA & THE SONG

(Ijangayanga - (Ij); and Ki (K))

Ij: Ki is that you? Is everybody ready?

K: Yes. Come on out. Everybody it's Ijangayanga!

Ij: Habari gani everybody! It's time to ring in the Kwanzaa day with my favorite song: Everywhere I Go, everybody's Talking About Kwanzaa. Okay now, let's get some clapping going…

K: What part do you want me to sing...tenor or bass?

Ij: Ki, I need you to take the Chisasi and keep the beat going. (He takes it) One-two! One-two! One-two!

K: Now what part do you want me to …..

Ij: Okay now, nobody forget your part… You're all going to sing, 'Everybody's talking About Kwanzaa!' Let's practice that...One-two go!

K: Okay, now what part do you want me to…

Ij: Ki, just shake the Chisasi...one-two! One-two! And kind of move your head while you're doing that!

K: Like this….

Ij: Perfect! Okay everyone, here we go!

K: What part do you want me to sing? Why do I think you don't want me to sing!

Ij: Wow! (to audience) He's really smart!

K: You don't want me to sing?

Ij: Ki, I saw the video of last year's Kwanzaa. You couldn't sing a high C or a low C...all you could sing was LOUSY.

K: I'm going to sing anyway....

Ij: Look here everybody, I need all of you to sing and drown him out!Let's do it!

(The song)

Ij: Great singing!

K: ………...and me/

Ij: Sorry, I've got to go! Bye!

K: I've got to go too! Good-bye everyone.

ME AND INDIA ROUTINE

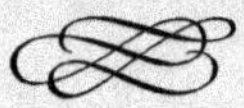

V: Tonight I'm going to tell a beautiful love story from India...the story of Moideen and Kanchanamala. We've been kind of busy trying to get ready...my partner and I. Oh P....

P: V.V.V...I couldn't do it. You've got to get your own food. I couldn't.

V: P....you didn't say "hello."

P: Hello. V. couldn't get what you asked for.

V: P., remember what I said, you're supposed to say hello in Hindi, the language of India.

P: Oh right...let me see...Hello - Hindi....Hindi - Hello... Hello ---Hindi....

I'm sorry my Hindi isn't handy.

V: It's 'Namested! Namested!'

P: Don't get upset with me!... I barely even know English.

V: Namested is how you say hello.

P: OOOOH! Okay then...YO everybody, Namested!

V: YO? That's not how one says it.

P: Well, I'm sorry, I'm India-ed out! I just couldn't get what you asked for.

V: I only asked you to buy food for the banquet.

P: Well, I got ' none (naan).'

V: Thanks, that's great! A few simple things to eat and you couldn't get them.

P: Why can't we just have regular food like jello. Everybody likes jello.

V: There's no such thing as "regular" food. If we were in France, fromage would be regular food. In Japan, sushi would be regular food; in west Africa, fofo; in Italy, pasta....

P: In America, "whatever is on the menu."

V: Look, I wanted everyone to share in the culture as I tell a story.

P: You needn't worry. By the time you're done, we'll all be sharing a nap.

V: Did you get some food or not?

P: I got None! (Naan)

V: We want to show the spices in Indian cuisine. The spices …

P: What? Cuisine?

V: Cuisine. India's cuisine --- foods.

P: This guy can't even talk regular.

V: I know all about cuisines. I used to train under a French chef at a four star restaurant.

P: I remember … .that was Mr. Pierre.

V: Right!

P: And you were Mr. Peuu!

V: Being a chef is an art. It takes a special skill. I'm not afraid to say that creative cooking is not my talent.

P: But you "are" afraid to say that storytelling is not your talent either. Tell them "that" and you will not be getting paid tonight.

V: Excuse me! I happen to be relatively famous for my storytelling!

P: I know, I know…"recognized by local doctors as the perfect cure for insomnia."

V: I wanted to show the spices of India. The food was important. The spices of India are world renowned. Everyone wanted those spices. I remember a certain Italian explorer back in 1492 who...

P: Oh a friend of yours?

V: Do I look like I was around in 1492?

P: --------------

V: Well?

P: I'm thinking it over.

V: I wasn't! I'm thinking about Christopher Columbus. Surely your history teacher told you about him.

P: My teacher's not 'Shirley (Surely),' it's Jim, and I wouldn't know. I sleep during that class.

V: Well Columbus was the first European in the 15th century to discover the "new world."

P: While looking for India. Right! I don't think that guy was listening in school either. "It's a whole different continent Chris!"

V: That's not the point...the point is...

P: The point is that he was trying to find a shortcut to India to get some spices and he ended up in a whole different place. Smart guy!

V: He was a smart guy. He was very smart.

P: Right. Let's say I'm a pilot and I'm going to fly you to New York and we end up in Washington….do you think anyone's going to say, 'Hey, that _(puppet name)... is smart? Or suppose Eon Musk takes a rocket and says he's going to Mars, and he lands on Saturn….do you think anybody's going to say, ' Wow! Smart guy!'

V: Look, I refuse to let you denigrate the Columbus name…

P: I knew it! You did know him!

V: Why are we talking about Columbus anyway. The question is 'Did you get the food that I asked for?'

P: I couldn't get it!

V: I sent you to the store. I gave you money! And you still didn't get it!

P: I got 'None.' None. They laughed at me when I tried to get it!

V: Laughed at you?

P: Yes, you asked me to get some shoe boxes. Nobody eats shoe boxes!

V: I didn't say "shoe boxes", I said get some Shuba.

P: Shuba? What's Shuba?

V: It's tomato soup with spices!

P: Oh no! I could have bought that!

V: And what did you get?

P: I got "none."

V: That doesn't help me my friend ... .I gave you money and a list…

P: You told me to buy an island, and they laughed at me! I didn't have enough money to buy an island.

V: An island? What island?

P: You told me to buy Samoa. I didn't have enough for that!

V: Samoa? I said, 'Get some "somoza."'

P: Samoza? What's that?

V: Samoza is a veggie dumpling. It's delicious!

P: Oh no! I could have bought it!

V: But you got "none."

P: Then you asked me to get some "mac and cheese." They don't sell mac and cheese there.

V: "Mac and cheese?" No, I said buy some "chicken makhani".

P: Chicken Makhani?

V: Yes, it's butter chicken. You like that!

P: Oh no! I could have got that! But I did get something…

V: You said that you got nothing…

P: No, I said that I got "none".

V: None!

P: None! It's flatbread from India…

V: Oh you mean "naan!"

P: None!

V: Naan!

P: None!

V: It's naan!

P: You say tomato! I say tomato!

V: Good, you bought some! We'll put some spices on it, and share it with everybody.

P: I did get you something else. I heard you talking on the telephone and you said that you needed a yoyo….so I got you a yoyo!

V: A yoyo? I never said that I wanted a yoyo……oh you heard me say that I wanted to get a yogi.

P: A yoyo.

V: Yogi.

P: Yoyo!

V: Yogi!

P: You say tomato, I say tomatoe! What's a yogi that a yoyo's not?

V: A yogi is a master of yoga. We were going to talk about yoga and do some exercises.

P: That's easy. You don't need a master for that, just put on some You-Tube videos. They've got yoga.

V: Oh no. People in American think yoga is just exercise, but in India yoga is a entire philosophy. It's got harmony, exercise and meditation…the ups and downs of life. I thought a yogi could help us with that.

P: What about the yoyo?

V: What about the yoyo?

P: The yoyo could help you with that stuff too. Yoyo's have harmony. It goes up and down.

In fact now that I think about it you should ask the yogi to get a Ugo Yoyo.

V: A Ugo yoyo?

P: Yes, from Utah. It's a little whistle-stop of a town called Yoyo.

V: A Ugo yoyo from Yoyo, Utah?

P: Yeah, ask the yogi about it. He'd like it….this yoyo does everything. It's got lights on it, it goes up and down, goes to sleep, walks the dog, goes over and under. Ask him.

V: I am not going to ask the yogi about a yoyo.

P: Well you're a "yoyo" if you don't ask the yogi about using the Ugo yoyo from Yoyo, Utah for yoga.

V: I can't even say it! Besides, the yogi is coming to show us how to meditate.

P: Meditate? Isn't that like sleep?

V: Well I suppose you might look at it like that….

P: If you want them to sleep, just tell them one of your stories.

V: Meditation involves a mantra…it's like a slogan you repeat over and over.

P: Even better. (to audience) I've got one for you guys, "Tell him to stop. Tell him to stop.

Tell him to stop!"

V: Do not take India's yoga lightly. It takes years to master…to become a yogi. I remember yoga in India goes back over 5000 years…

P: Don't tell me, you knew the first yogi.

V: Do I look like I knew the first yogi…..don't answer that!

P: I was going to say "No." The second --- a definite "maybe."

V: Did you do what I asked you to do?

P: What's that?

V: The song?

P: Wait, I do have something…..I got a DVD at the Flea Market. It's Bollywood.

V: You've got a Bollywood DVD? Bollywood and musical entertainment from India? You? Isn't that a little high class for you?

P: No. I'll have you know I'm a very cultured dog. I'm part French Poodle, part German Shepherd, part English Bulldog, Zimbabwean Hound and part Mexican Chihuahua. I'm a real mutt.

V: There's nothing Indian in any of those.

P: Oh, but I have a wee bit of Bengal Tiger in me.

V: Bengal Tiger?

P: Yep!

V: But that's impossible! Tigers and dogs can't get together.

P: Yep! I know. That's just what my mom said……she made a mistake.

V: (pause) And….

P: And?

V: What happened?

P: Oh nothing. The tiger's claws were too long and he was too clingy.

V: Never mind…just give us the song from India. Did you learn a song from Bollywood?

P: Well no, but I do have another song from …near India.

V: Near India?

P: Yeah…. Indiana. I've got a song from Indiana. "Take Me Out to the Ball Game."

V: Baseball? They don't play baseball in India, they play cricket .

P: I don't care. They can play with whatever team they want….the crickets, grasshoppers, the daddy long legs….it's all baseball.

V: Just sing.

(They sing)

MUSICAL INTRODUCTION

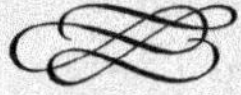

V: ….and now I'd like to bring out one of my instruments….

D: Thanks. I've never been called an instrument before.

V: Everyone, this is my friend Kit, the dog.

D: What are you doing up here?

V: I was getting ready to play a drum….

D: Where is Mr. KDN, the drummer.

V: I'm not sure. I haven't seen him.

D: You can't play the drum!

V: I know. Need I remind you….I have an accordion.

D: You can't play the accordion either.

V: What are you talking about? I was a prodigy.

D: Take that up with a medical doctor, I'm talking about your playing.

V: Kit, remember, accordion playing runs in my family.

D: Yeah, I know….when you start playing everybody runs…away.

V: Don't put my playing down!

D: I'm not putting your playing down….I just want you to put that accordion down.

V: Why should I? The apple doesn't fall far from the tree. My great grandfather played the accordion; my grandfather played the accordion; my father played the accordion….

D: And then you happened.

V: I was the apple of their eye! Not far from the tree at all!

D: Well, that apple that was you…fell from the tree….then rolled down a hill…..straight into a gully!

V: Look….I can play! I play all the keys… I can play high C….I can play Middle C….I can play Low C

D: And through it all, you still play Lousy.

V: I had lessons. I had homework. All of those books…I had homework in Book A, Book B, Book D.

D: Book D, what happened to Book C?

V: The dog ate it.

D: Oh yeah, I forgot. It taste pretty good....way better than your playing. What made you decide to bring out that accordion again.

V: Well, I tried it when I was younger, but I had a lot of responsibilities so I gave it up. But I've been looking around, and I think it's time I gave it a shot.

D: I think you've had too many shots.

V: I could have been on America's Got Talent.

D: No. You could have been on their sister show.

V: Their sister show?

D: Yes, American's Got The Talentless too.

V: Don't forget I played before four presidents.

D: _____, practicing in front of Mount Rushmore doesn't count.

V: I'm playing!

D: I'm going!

V: Wait! Don't go...why don't you do something for everyone.

D: Me?

V: YOU.

D: We'll, I guess I could do a little something…

THE BANKING ROUTINE

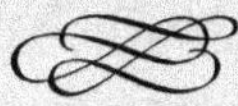

V: Good Evening ladies and gentlemen. It's wonderful to be here today.

F: Right. What a dump!

V: What? You don't walk into somebody's space and call it a dump. It's rude. It's crud. You didn't even say 'Hello.'

F: Oh, excuse me....Hello! How's everybody doing?.......Good....This place is a dump! And before ________ here tells me to say 'I'm sorry,' I'll beat him to it myself and say it...'I'm sorry...this place is a dump!'

V: What's wrong with you? What are you doing?

F: I hope we're getting paid for this.

V: What do you care if we're getting paid? You'll get your

cut. You're always worried about Money. You don't see me worried about money.

F: Yeah, that's the problem….YOU don't worry about money. I have needs!

V: What, another video game? That's the problem with you and your generation, you're too soft. You don't know sacrifice….you don't know struggle. Why when I was young I was very poor….but after years of effort, years of struggle and sacrifice….

F: You're still poor.

V: I don't like to say 'poor'…I live 'comfortably.'

F: Yeah, YOUR fancy way to say…POOR.

V: We don't live so badly.

F: Really? We're both living out of suitcases. Where are we anyway? (to audience) Where are we? What city?

(answer)

F: Oh no! We're on hard times again! We were in Vegas, New York, D.C. and now _________. What's next? _________(name a nearby small town)?

V: Will you calm down….

F: We need an investment! We should have invested our money. You need an investment.

V: Well, I'm open to investing.

F: Oh really? You'll let me invest your money?

V: If it's a worthwhile investment… I'm open. Unlike you, I know about money. I learned from Benjamin Franklin.

F: Benny Franklin? You know Benny Franklin?

V: Everyone knows Ben Franklin. He's famous!

F: Are we talking about the same person?

V: I'm talking about the Ben Franklin with the pithy statements….like 'a penny saved is a penny earned.'

F: A penny? That ain't Benny! Benny said, ' an apple a day… will keep you ….on the toilet.'

V: Ben Franklin was in a band of patriots.

F: Yeah, that's him. He's the lead guitar in the band Stars and Stripes.

V: Ben Franklin lived in 1776.

F: No. Benny lives in 17E over on 21st Street.

V: I'm talking about Benjamin Franklin from the American Revolution in 1776. In fact there were two Bennies…I mean Benjamin's. There was Benjamin Banneker, the genius architect and Benjamin Franklin, the genius inventor.

F: What? And you knew them? No wonder you're standing here talking about pennies…you're old!

V: Franklin the man was very wise….'A penny saved is a penny earned.'

F: WE don't do pennies….WE do CashApp. Benny Franklin used to be my Uber driver. You should meet him. He'll show you how to invest your money.

V: Right, an Uber driver.

F: He's an investment banker.

V: Oh great! An investment banker by day and an Uber driver by night….how successful can he be?

F: This from someone who saves….pennies?

V: I just want to know. If I'm giving you my money to invest I think I have the right to know who you're investing with.

F: Oh you're reminding me of my sister.

V: Your sister?

F: Yeah. She said she doesn't trust me with her money. She thinks I'll give it all away along with her passwords. She doesn't even think I respect her privacy.

V: Well at least she was honest. It was nice of her to tell you.

F: She didn't. I read it in her diary. Now getting back to your investments……

V: 'Investment(s)'……with an 'S'. I'm not investing with someone I don't know.

F: You're not. You're investing with me. Benny gave me the rules of being an investment banker. Rule one: If you use your own money, you're considered a genius and an entrepreneur.

V: And rule two….

F: Never use your own money…..use other people's money!

V: And if you use other people's money?

F: Then you are a 'broker'….. And they are the 'brokee.'

V: So I'm going to be 'broke.' No thank you.

F: It's better you than me. Wait. You really need to give my guy Benny a chance. He can find us some good investments.

V: Alright. So where is he? Is he driving Uber right now?

F: No. He stopped driving after the robbery.

V: Robbery? He got robbed?

F: The bank got robbed. He was in the bank one day

when it got robbed. Guy demanded all the money....'put it in a bag and hand it over.'

V: Was he scared?

F: No. According to him, he didn't flinch.

V: That's amazing. He's both lucky and bold.

F: Yeah, that's what the police said.....when they arrested him outside. Said he was bold for trying to rob that bank and lucky that explosive money pack hadn't gone off.

V: Your friend is a bank robber?

F: If it's any consolation, he said the bank robbed him first....all of those fees. You can meet him in about 10 years. .

V: No thanks. I'll stick with the original Ben Franklin.

F: But you don't follow Ben Franklin's example.

V: What do you mean?

F: 'A penny saved is a penny earned.' You know he saved a penny a day. Died with 10 thousand pennies. So the bank put his name and face on the hundred dollar bill. The only bill that has your name on it is your credit card bill. They called. They wanted to know about your investment too.

V: My investment?....... Don't tell me you used my credit card to invest money....don't tell me you used my credit card to invest money!

F: Okay. Okay. Since you insist… I won't tell you. Just make sure you call them tomorrow between 9 And 5. Ask for Ms. Gengis Khan, and be prepared to be 'the brokee.'

V: What did you do? What did you do?

F: Well I took your card and bought 50 shares at 50 dollars a share.

V: What?

F: Things were going great! First it went up to 55 dollars a share.

V: Fifty-five dollars?

F: Then it went down to forty-eight.

V: Forty-eight? That's bad.

F: Then it went up to fifty-one…..

V: Well that's good. Fifty-one…

F: Then it went sneaking down to twenty-two.

V: Twenty-two?

F: Then it bounced up to thirty.

V: It bounced ….good!

F: Then it fell…down…..

V: Down?…..

F: Down……

V: Down?…….

F: Down…….

V: Down?……down…..to?….

F: One.

V: One?….. One dollar?

F: No…..One penny.

V: What? A penny? I have a penny stock now?

F: It's okay!….. You like pennies! You and Ben Franklin. Maybe you should have followed the advice of that other Benjamin, the architect Benjamin Banneker.

V: What did he say?

F: Forget pennies. If you're investing, only invest in real estate.

THE TOOTH FAIRY

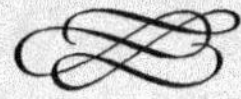

T: I'm done!

V: Hey, everyone….we have a special guest! It's the Tooth Fairy! (takes her out)

T: Great introduction. Thanks for the weak applause. It's okay…I'm used to silence. I work in the dark.

V: Well how are you doing?

T: I'm done! That's how I'm doing….I'm done!

V: You seem upset. What happened?

T: Kids today! That's what happened…Kids today!

V: Kids today?

T: Kids today don't appreciate! Back in the day, I'd take that old nasty tooth they'd leave under the pillow. I'd leave them a penny and they'd smile. Leave them a nickel and they'd giggle. Leave them a quarter and they'd say they were rich. And a dollar? You'd think they had a gold tooth! But not today!

I left some kid a dollar and he wakes up and says, 'YO! Why can't I get 10?'

V: Why can't I get 10?

T: 'YO!' 'Why can't I get 10?' I had to stop myself. I was gonna say, 'YO! You want 10? Let me back hand your smart mouth and knock out 9 more!' Had to stop myself.

V: What happened to 'sugar and spice and everything nice?'

T: Not today! Today it's dog-eat-dog!

V: That's so cynical…that's so skeptical….that's so…

T: 2024! I've decided to give it up. I'm retiring.

V: But who's going to take your place?

T: CashApp. I'm gonna let it all go…do something new.

V: What about the kids?

T: They'll be disappointed…which kids? My kids?

V: You have kids?

T: I have three. They're all grown….two boys and a girl. The oldest son decided to follow in my footsteps.

V: Oh, he's a tooth fairy?

T: No, a dentist. My daughter became a ballerina.....invites me every year to see her dance the Sugar Plum Fairy in the Nut Cracker.

V: And the other boy?

T: He's a bum.

He takes after his father…my second husband. I should have known that marriage wasn't going to last. The day we got married I heard him say to the minister…'Well Rev., one man's trash is another man's treasure.' That was a red flag. You may have heard of him….the Sandman.

V: The Sandman?

T: Yeah, does absolutely nothing but throw sand everywhere. The house is a mess. I should have married the bunny.

V: The bunny? You mean the Easter Bunny?

T: At least he keeps you hopping! (laughs)

V: You mean all of those characters are real? …….Did you ever meet Santa?

T: Oh him!….we dated a few times before he married Martha. It didn't work out. That guy has a sugar addiction. You know he has no teeth.

V: No teeth? But you have yours?

T: I have all of mine. I count them every night when I take them out.

V: Oh my.

T: But it's all going to change. I'm retiring.

V: What are you going to do?

T: I don't know, I've never retired before. What do "people" do when they retire?

V: Some like to travel. You could take a cruise.

T: A cruise? Why would I take a cruise, I can fly!.....of course I don't fly in bad weather any more….

V: Oh, turbulence?

T: No, arthritis. My body doesn't like bad weather. In fact I know when the bad weather is coming before the weatherman.

V: Before?

T: Yes, everything starts hurting. ….In fact if it doesn't hurt, it doesn't work.

V: Well some people like to do gardening when they retire. You could be a farmer.

T: You know about farming? Where?

V: I grew up on a farm, but today I live in the city. I, like many others, have a container garden.

T: A container garden? You're growing containers?

V: No, no. You get yourself a large pot……

T: Oh, I know about 'pot.' I smoke it every week. It helps my nerves.

V: I'm not talking about Marijuana, I'm talking about a flower pot. You plant seeds in it….like tomatoes.

T: I do like tomatoes.

V: Of course if you plant tomatoes, you need to get a stake.

T: Oh I do love steak and tomatoes too. Delicious!

V: No, not a steak. When I say 'a stake,' I don't mean 'a steak,' I mean 'a stake.'

T: When you say 'a steak,' you don't mean 'a steak,' you mean 'a steak!' ….and what have you been smoking?

V: I'm talking about a stake….a stick….you put it in the pot to let the tomatoes run. You know tomatoes run.

T: (makes a face) Oh right, right…..heaven forbid they walk.

V: I give up. Forget farming. You could just write a book

about your experiences. I'm sure you've had lots of experiences.

T: Have I ever! You'd be surprised what you run into when you go into people's houses at night. Some of those people became famous, and I was there.

V: Famous? Like who?

T: Oh, there were lots of people. I can always tell who's going to be a winner and who's going to be a loser.

V: Really? What about me? Did you know what I would be when I was little?

T: Who are you again?

V: I'm ________________________.

T: Oh yes! Didn't you live at ____________________ in ____________________. The big house with all the rooms?

V: Yes, that was mine.

T: Didn't you have ___ brothers and sisters living with you?

V: Yes. Yes, that's me. Did you see me becoming a winner or a loser?

T: Aren't you a ventriloquist today?

V: Yes, yes! So what did you think?

T: I didn't think you'd get this far…………..but congratulations on your retirement!

V: But I'm not retired.

T: Oh, but you should be.

THE WRITER

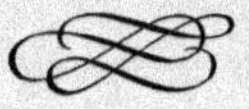

IJ: How do you spell "cat."

Ki: C - A - T.

Ij: How do you spell "eat?"

Ki: E - A - T .

Ij: How do you spell "seat?"

Ki: What are you doing?

Ij: It's my newest "thing!" I always have a "thing."

Ki: I know...there's always a "thing" with you. So what thing is this?

Ij: I'm a writer. I write. I'm writing a book.

Ki: You? Well that's nice. What genre are you using?

Ij: Genre? Oh no, I'm just using an ink pen.

Ki: No, I'm asking what kind of book you're writing. Is it sci-fi, mystery, romance, history…?

Ij: It's recipe. I'm writing a cook book.

Ki: Is this your first book? Cook books are the hardest books to write.

Ij: No, it's easy, you just put some recipes in.

Ki: No, a good cook book is a travelogue.

Ij: A what?

Ki: A travelogue! A travelogue!

Ij: Astalavista to you too!

Ki: What are you talking about….a travelogue means you have to write about the place the foods come from.

Ij: The places?

Ki: The place…if you're writing about Japanese cuisine, you have to write about places in Japan.

South African cuisine….places you've been in South Africa. Italian…places in Italy. You have to write about the place. So what place are these recipes from?

Ij: McDonald's.

Ki: McDonald's! McDonald's food is already cooked.

Ij: My recipes are on the sauces….Barbeque, Sweet and Sour, Honey Mustard….did you know if you mix them all together they taste like garbage?

Ki: Garbage? Who would want a cook book that says that? Garbage, who eats garbage?

Ij: My nana.

Ki: I know your grandmother, and she does not eat garbage!

Ij: I didn't say my granny, I said my nana…that's my goat. She loves garbage.

Ki: If you have a goat, why don't you come up with recipes for goat's milk.

Ij: Goat's milk! Eeugh!

Ki: So exactly what recipes are you putting in this book?

Ij: Jello.

Ki: Jello?

Ij: Jello. Did you know that there are 26 kinds of jello? I've got all kinds of jello recipes…. Macaroni and jello. Ravioli and jello…. Spaghetti and jello…..cheese and…

Ki: Jello?

Ij: Don't be ridiculous! They don't go together.

Ki: I think your book needs an editor.

Ij: An editor?

Ki: There's a lot of rejection in being a writer. You have to be able to take rejection. You send it in….they send it back. You send it in…they send it back…you send it in….

Ij: It's a book…not a dinner at McDonald's.

Ki: You send things back at McDonald's?

Ij: All the time. I want it right.

Ki: But everything is cooked the same at McDonald's.

Ij: I know, that's the problem. I want frozen hamburgers, they won't give it to me.

Ki: Frozen?

Ij: Yeah, they're good with Jello.

Ki: Nonetheless what I think you need is an editor to help your book.

Ij: An editor?

Ki: Yes, a good editor.

Ij: Naturally you have one.

Ki: Yes, I do.

Ij: It's you isn't it.

Ki: Well, yes. I know all about editing.

Ij: Is there nothing you don't know? Or are you trying to squeeze in on my profits?

Ki: Profits? That shows you know nothing about writing. There's no profits in book writing unless you are at the top or you are dead.

Ij: Naturally you know that too...which one are you?

Ki: I'm not at the top.

Ij: Yeah, I thought you were dead.

Ki: Look, do you want an editor or not?

Ij: Okay, I guess. If I don't like it, you'll be fired.

Ki: Good. Now just give me your book and I'll go through it.

Ij: Okay, it's right here…. (book shown)

Ki: There's nothing in here. It's only got one sentence! I can't edit one sentence.

Ij: You're fired!

PART IV

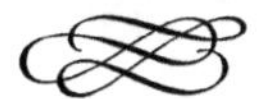

GOING PRO...THERE IS NO BUSINESS LIKE SHOW BUSINESS

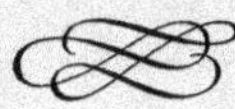

It's not easy....but going back to the title of that Orben book....IF YOU HAVE TO BE A COMIC. Replace the word COMIC with VENTRILOQUIST. Now stop and take a deep breath....and think...do you really have to be a ventriloquist?

Take a moment...think of all of the superhero comics or movies that you've seen. (There aren't that many women....if you are a woman. There aren't that many gays...if you are gay.) Don't think about the hero parts, think about their secret identities...the complicated lives they live. Can our hero be married? Have children? What kind of family life? Now take a deep breath and think about yourself. That complicated secret identity life is what you are going to have. The show biz is the "superhero" life, but when you are "not working" (HA! HA! HA!) what kind of mundane life will you encounter.

If you are really into family stuff, you need to reconsider. Family events, friend events, weddings, funerals, graduations, your kid's stuff, holidays, etc., etc. are all on the chopping block often at the last minute. You (the superhero) have "work" to do….it's not always about performing….you'll have meetings, rehearsals, practices, PR sessions, telephone calls, video conference calls, ETC., ETC. (Notice I'm making these "etc.,etc"s bigger, because they have to be more important if you want to stay a pro.) Saving the world with your art has to be more important than anything or anyone else in your life! Period!

My favorite uncle stopped talking to me years ago. He's never forgiven me…and I'm still hurting. He drove from another state to see my mother and I. He arrived by noon and stayed until dusk. I didn't have performances that day, I had meetings that day with producers hence I was not carrying the show bags. When I arrived (bagless) he was literally walking off the porch… leaving. I only had time to say "hello"…..and he's never forgiven me for disrespecting him by not stopping "my busy day" to see him. It still hurts. This was the uncle who encouraged me. He was the one who shared my silly riddles and jokes with his sailor buddies on the ship when I'd write to him at 10 years old. And yet, if I had to do that day over…..I'd still go to the meetings! That's what it takes to be a pro. I got a call the other day….a Christmas Eve show? During the evening… a party of 50….."I'll take it!" My family has already planned an event…they expect me to be there, but I won't be! I have to work...my job is to make "other" people happy first....and yes, that's what it takes to be a pro!

Take a deep breath and think about that. What does it take...IF YOU HAVE TO BE A COMIC....IF YOU HAVE TO BE A VENTRILOQUIST?

What is your breaking point? If you can confidently say "there isn't one! I HAVE TO DO THIS!"........ then you are ready.

ME, MYSELF, AND I

I was an amateur ventriloquist and puppeteer growing up. I started practicing and creating when I was six. My parents thought that I would grow out of it. They refused to buy me a little Danny O Day figure for years! They finally relented when I was in eighth grade. I got him for Christmas. Finally! In 9th grade, I made my first full figure. (Thanks Paul Winchell for your book's instructions.) I became a semi-pro after college. I lived and worked in Harrisburg, PA. I was a teacher and I worked at a fast-food restaurant in the evenings. As a teacher I was able to take a few gigs at various schools and weekend events. Birthday parties became a thing as well. My fast food work also allowed me to perform at parties held in the restaurant much to the delight of the manager. He was able to promote that there was a ventriloquist magician available for any party booked there. I enjoyed Harrisburg, but I was ready to move on. I realized that I could not go pro in a small city, I needed a larger space for performing. I moved back to Philadelphia, so I decided to take the leap! I've never looked back.

There were a few moments when I wondered if it was worth it, and I can count those moments on one hand… like the time I got banned from performing for the U.S. military for insulting "a general" at a show. They called and asked for an African-American History show. Why me? A recommendation. I'm a comic and ventriloquist storyteller! Their only caveat…make sure the show was educational as "general so-and-so" had been the guest lecturer that last year and so they wanted something equally educational. I worked for a month on their little presentation. I think they would have liked it. Would have! But then they did the unforgivable! It is the one thing that enrages me, and always gets me into trouble….they called me two days before the show to ask about the content of the show. "Is it going to be good? Is it going to be okay… because general so-and-so is going to be there." How do I explain this…as a performer…as a comedian….my response to this kind of action is always the same…and yes, this kind of thing has happened a few times in my life. I DON'T RECOMMEND THIS TO OTHERS. IT'S JUST A "ME" THING. If a sponsor has hired me and asked for a particular show and I've spent weeks creating it….don't call me a few days before the show to ask about the content! I look at it like "you hired ME, you know what you're getting." When that second call is made, my anger mounts. I throw the script away (and using the skill from the exercises given in this little booklet), I write an entirely new show (in a day) .....making that person or persons a target! OUCH! For this particular show, I threw out all of the history content and told the story of JACK AND THE BEANSTALK. When I was done, "general so-and-so" and the sponsors were embarrassed....beet red! On the other hand, I got a standing ovation! (As of this writing, I've had three in my career.) I had a show at the Willow Grove Air base later that year. I was dressed and ready to go. When my mother heard where I was going, she just laughed and said it would be a wasted trip. She was right...I was denied entry. Oh well! Lesson learned? NAH! But in spite of the few hic-cups, I have been in as a pro over thirty years.

My workday is 12 - 15 hours. Show business is just that.... 50% show and 50% business ... .so I do the business part for 6 hours and the art part for 6 hours. Minimums.

The business side consists of researching venues to perform, writing emails to sponsors, mailing e-brochures to client lists, telephone calls of all natures, reading the trades and having meetings with anyone I think can help me in my journey. Read Joel Bauer's book: HUSTLE, HUSTLE. Yes, 32 phone calls...yes it works. I also have to keep the ledger up to date. Make sure the back-up systems are completed, i.e. hand write or print out the calendars and the show information in case the computer networks go down. (Been there.)

The art side consists of practicing (technique stuff), rehearsing the scripts, writing jokes, writing scripts, making the puppets, making the props, studying the arts in books and YouTube videos, reviewing works of others, reviewing my own work with the industry's standards, shopping for bargains which I can use in the shows. I also take time to meet and be friends with other artists. Sharing a laugh or sob story with my peers is just as fun as curling up in a corner at 2:00 am to read a history book or a biography.

I think that if one wants to be a pro, one should define what success means to oneself as the journey begins. When I was a teen, I decided that I didn't want "national" fame…local fame would be fine. I liked Lee Dexter and his work. He was on a local channel with "Bertie the Bunyip." He was a great ventriloquist and I loved his puppets growing up. I saw him riding down the street with Bertie in a Thanksgiving Day Parade and was so happy when he seemed to wave at me. (Okay, I know now!) I never wanted to be BIG like Paul Winchell, or Shari Lewis. So "local" was the road I pursued and I'm content with where it has led. Television and radio…been there. Major performer in the area…yes! Local celebrity….yes! Regional performer….yes, I'm a hundred miler (as Ken and Roberta Griffith defined it). I perform all over the region, but not far enough away that I need to sleep in hotels or motels between dates. Money in the bank....well, it's never enough, but I'm not homeless (yet)...the puppets are happy! So I'm happy too. To be a pro...find your niche!

THE SHOW

I won't give you pipe dreams, so suffice it to say that my programs are interdisciplinary. I have my puppets and a figure along with my accordion, and my magical illusions. I tell stories in the show as well. My regular show is 45- 50 minutes long.

If I'm on a bill with other performers, I generally have 20 minutes to work. I use two puppets for that kind of set.

If the sponsor books me for 60 - 90 minutes or more, I bring in other artists. These are friends who I've worked with in the past or the artists I've mentored (son # 1). The show will allow for an opening act or a middle act with my artist friend. I will carry the bulk of the show. My artist friends include magicians, balloon artists, drummers and poets.

I have never tried to do a 90 minute or longer set alone. I've never filled a stadium or a large 1000 plus seat auditorium. The largest venue I've had was 800, and the smallest was with one (a child, post-op and in bed). My average audience size is 50 - 200. I have performed in clubs, churches, outdoor picnics, yachts, festivals, schools, libraries, museums, rehab centers, senior centers and houses. I enjoy these types of programs. I have never done corporate events such as a trade show nor have I performed on "major" cruises. They don't interest me. I have never entered competitions such as America's Got Talent, and such events don't interest me. I stopped doing television. I just got tired of the whole format ... .Television is an all day "thing" for your 5 - 10 minutes....I just have other things I could be doing. Is it worth it? Yes and No. People do see your appearance and they may remember it for a week...and then? Forgotten! Why not just mount a YouTube or TikTok video...which allows you to control the production values as well as your time.

TIPS...THE LITTLE THINGS DO MATTER

Remember it's all about the comedy.....

Go slower! Wait for the laughs, then start again just as the laughs go down.

Comedy has a rhythm. Don't rush your sets.

Analyze your show after each one....and write down your thoughts in a notebook so you can review them through the years.

Make up rules as you learn....and follow them. Adapt

other performers' Rules and make them your own as well to avoid chaos.

Take me for example:

I get stage fright before every performance....YES, EVERY PERFORMANCE! I found a paper on "Preventing Stage Fright" and have continued to do what it said. So I have a routine to calm me down...I do at least 10 Jumping Jacks while waiting. I do 10 minutes of vent lip control before a mirror or on my telephone to keep my lips from quivering as I start. Just before going on I look out at the audience and whisper, "I love you! I love you all!"

Some of my rules over the years:

a. Gas up the car at night....you won't have time to stop in the morning.

b. Set the show the night before....you won't have time in the morning.

c. Arrive early at least an hour if traveling to another city ....One time I was distracted the night before, but had a school show at 10:00am. in Atlantic City. I jumped out of bed late at 8:00am, rushed, and away I drove. I arrived at the school at 9:00 am (8:45 am to be exact). Opened the trunk to discover an empty space....I had forgotten to load the show! No time to panic....I drove over to a Dollar Store grabbed everything I needed to mount a show. I returned to the school with 15 minutes to set. A harrowing experience, but the shows were successful…(I presented an Anansesum…for those that don't know, it's traditional African theater piece with Ananse the spider. It wasn't what I had planned, but it worked!) The lesson for me…don't be distracted and don't rush.

d. Put the show away (i.e. pack for the next performance) before leaving the site to avoid leaving props….little props have a way of hiding. Things I've left and had to go back for: a camel bell, an egg bag, a squirrel puppet, a J& G bag, a Palmo.

e. Always carry the portable mike system. Make sure it's fully charged….I had a birthday party and surprise! It was in a large hall. The mike was a life saver…so I always carry it now.

f. Place scented soaps in the cases especially during summer….your hands and arms sweat….the puppets/figures get sweaty and if you're touring they can smell. Clean them when you can, but the scented soaps work wonders.

g. Turn your costumes inside out when storing…keeps the light from fading the colors.

h. No matter how long the day, take time to rehearse and take time to write jokes and/or routines.

JOKE STEALING

Ventriloquists are known for stealing each other's materials. The problem is that it is done so often that the material is "old" and out-dated. When I read some of the printed dialogue books, I just shake my head as the authors never acknowledge their source material....the original ventriloquist and his/her partner! I was appalled to see one ventriloquist win America's Got Talent as he weekly presented other people's material. It's not very professional, but some of us ventriloquists do have "class." In stand-up...if you steal, you definitely get called out and sometimes beat up! That offense is not tolerated in the stand-up comedy world. Personally I think one a bit arrogant to think that this or that joke was one's own creation. We live on a planet with billions of people. History has shown "simultaneous" development of major projects....the Wright Brothers were working on an airplane at the same time as someone in France. Lest we forget, there was Tesla and Edison working on electricity. A joke is merely a "word play". The U.S.A. has 250 million people. Are you telling me that YOU alone could come up with a "word play," and NO ONE ELSE could have the same concept? Now I'm laughing.

This little booklet has been made to help you avoid that "old tired routine" from the past and to avoid stealing other people's current material. If you do feel the need to utilize someone else's jokes, do me one small favor…..acknowledge that person at the end of your show. When the applause is ending….and you are saying "THANK YOU. THANK YOU." to your audience. Add another line. Just say, "…and a special thanks to (his/her last name) for helping with the material." (if that person is alive)

And if that person has passed away…." and a special thanks to ___________________ and his/her partner ___________________."

Trust me, if that living person hears about it, he or she won't be as mad…because you've acknowledged them. On the other hand the deceased ventriloquist's family will be honored that you've mentioned their loved one in your ending. Everyone's happy and you won't be accused of stealing.

MY CONCLUSIONS

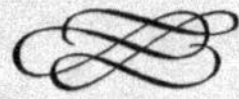

Comedy is a serious business, but I can't take it seriously all of the time. We comics do have an important role to play in this world. We help people "live." Our animal brothers and sisters can play with each other and even play with us, but they don't tell jokes. They don't tell stories or remember punch lines. Hence they can't build civilizations. They can't build a house out of stone, build cars or computers because they can't remember and pass on the methods. They can't make fun of people or methods of building things which help us reinforce the hows in building things. Only people can. I never forget that there are some jobs which are more important than mine…..a doctor, a surgeon, a surveyor, a bricklayer, etc. I guess there is a hierarchy of jobs, but being a ventriloquist is definitely on that list somewhere.

And speaking of somewhere…. our planet is one of

mystery. It remains a part of a vast universe of planets and stars. Everyday it seems that some person goes missing....he or she disappears from the planet. The Missing 411 Series by David Paulidas documents cases of missing people. Dr. David Jacobs has a book series that speculates on the pesky extraterrestrials' involvement in abducting people from our planet. The earth is one planet among millions across the universe. I'm a believer in extraterrestrial visits. Afterall, where are these missing people? Where have they gone? These are people of every nationality, every occupation....where are they? I pray for them everyday. Seriously, I do. I'm also sure that one (or two) of them is a ventriloquist and as I look up at the stars, I think that they may be out there somewhere....doing what we have to do. Somewhere among the stars are "people" making puppets and using them to make others laugh....there is no choice... they have to.....just as we have to....because we just have to be ventriloquists.

Now fill out the form:

Place of birth: <u>EARTH</u>

Occupation: <u>VENTRILOQUIST</u>